Up the Missouri

John Brickwedel

UP THE MISSOURI

By John Brickwedel

John Brickwedel

Up The Missouri

Copyright © 2024 by **John Brickwedel**

All rights reserved. No part of this book may be reproduced or transmitted, downloaded, distributed, reverse engineered, or stored in or introduced into any information storage and retrieval system, in any form or by any means, including photocopying and recording, whether electronic or mechanical, now known or hereinafter invented without permission in writing from the publisher.

DISCLAIMER: The contents of this work, including, but not limited to, the accuracy of events, people, and places depicted; opinions expressed; permission to use previously published materials included; and any advice given or actions advocated are solely the responsibility of the author, who assumes all liability for said work and indemnifies the publisher against any claims stemming from publication of the work.

To order additional copies of this book, please contact:

MAPLE LEAF PUBLISHING INC.
www.mapleleafpublishinginc.com

General Inquiries & Customer Service
Phone: 1-(403)-356-0255
Email: info@mapleleafpublishinginc.com

ISBN Paperback: 978-1-77419-215-3
ISBN eBook: 978-1-77419-214-6

Table of Contents

Copyright 3
Table of Contents 4
THE FLOWER GIRL 6
THE VOYAGE 32
BOSTON 41
BALTIMORE 52
TO THE OHIO RIVER 66
THE BOAT 85
THE TRIP 100
THE FORT 117
THE VISITORS 131
THE SIOUX 135
THE CAPTAIN'S STORY 146
THE WINTER 150
RENDEZVOUS 171
THE HOMECOMING 183
GOOD TIMES 190
ST. LOUIS 209
GOING BACK HOME 227
THE SECOND WINTER 253

There are a lot of stories about the early settlers to the west. Some of them are true. The mountain men were the first to come to stay. Most of them did not bring wives. Most took wives from one tribe or another and were called squaw men. Some did bring wives from back east. Those were traders who worked for one fur trading company or another and had a more settled way of life and even a cabin to live in.

This story is historically correct but is fiction, therefore the names used are also fictitious. The names of the places I took from an old map. The place I chose for their post is by the town of Columbus, Montana.

The Author.

CHAPTER ONE
THE FLOWER GIRL

The young man watched out the window of the inn as the midday traffic hurried by. He was tall for those days, a little over six feet. He was broad at the shoulder and narrow at the hip, as Zane Gray always said. His father had built up a general merchandise business and brought his son in as an apprentice when he was twelve. He had gone to a good school for five years before that.

His name was John Brix of Brix and Son General Merchandise Co. When his father thought he was old enough the two of them went to Boston and opened a store for him to run. That was in 1816 at the end of the war, and it was safe again to ship what was needed for a store. Maybe 20 years old was a little too soon to run a business, but so far it had worked.. Then he received a message from the business manager of his father's store in London that his father was sick and was failing; he was instructed to hurry home. He left his business in the hands of his store manager and hurriedly packed to leave Boston for London. He went first to the banker to draw out enough money for the trip, next down to the shipping company that he used to bring in the goods that he had shipped over from England. He and his father did not own their own vessel. They only had one general merchandise store in London and his store in Boston. And during the war between England and the U.S.A. there had been a lot of ships lost to privateers. His father thought it better to let someone else take the risk.

The clerk took him right to the manager's office and knocked on the door. Mr. Warner called "Come in." The clerk announced "Mr. Brix, sir." Standing, Mr. Warner said, "Come in, Mr. Brix, I hope the day finds you in good health."

"My health is fine, thank you, but the business that brought me here is another matter. Do you have a ship sailing for London in the near future?"

"I do. We have one loading now. It will be ready to sail in two days."' "Good, I would like to book passage if you have space."

Mr. Warner picked up some papers from his desk and looked them over; "Yes, I thought so, at this point in time with the war over for so short a period not a lot of traffic to London. Still some bad feelings you know. Well, she will be sailing on the evening tide in two days so you should board by noon. And if you want good food to eat you had better bring it with you."

Mr. Brix paid for his passage and told Mr. Warner of the sickness of his father and assured him that he would still be shipping with him. At the suggestion of the shipping agent he arranged for a box of food to take with him on the ship.

The crossing was a little stormy but otherwise uneventful. On arriving in London he found his father had passed on. After the legal paperwork was finished, he went to work selling the business and his father's house and furnishings then he rented rooms at an inn. While sitting at a table by a window his attention was suddenly taken by a young girl selling flowers outside the window of the inn. She was being accosted by two sailors who had had too much to drink. He went outside and asked the girl if she needed help. One of the sailors turned at his approach. "We're just havin' a little fun so bugger off, boy, less you are married to her or something." Just then a watchman with a big heavy staff came up and asked, "Is everything alright, Margaret?" She answered, "Those two clods ruined my flower tray and tore my scarf. They have made me lose a whole day's pay." She had a soft but forceful voice that he liked. The watchman asked, "How much will you lose?"

"'If I sold all the flowers that they wrecked it would be more than a pound."

"Well, sea dogs, pay up or off you go to jail." The two sailors looked like they were about to contest the issue when our hero stepped up and said, "If you will accept two pounds for your flowers I will take them all. "The watchman asked, "Who are you and what have you to do with all this?"

"My name is John Brix and I was coming to this young lady's aid when you showed up."

The young lady responded, "That, sir, is very kind of you but are you sure?"

"If you will allow me to I will be most happy to buy them."

The watchman said, "Do you two gentlemen of the sea still want to go to jail or are we through here?" The two sailors just growled something and turned and walked away. The watchman watched as John paid the girl the two pounds then bid them a good day and walked on up the street.

John said, "I see that you have friends here and that you probably didn't need my help but it gave me a chance to talk to you. You have a sign on your flower tray saying that you do sewing or are you just advertising for someone else?"

"No, I do it myself."

"Good. If you would come have a cup of tea with me, I would like to talk to you about sewing."

She smiled. "Did you want a dress made for you? I don't think I would have a pattern that would fit those broad shoulders." Laughing, they went inside to the table that he had just left.

When the innkeeper came over John ordered some tea and a cold lunch. "I myself have not had any breakfast yet. I hope you will feel free to join me."

"I haven't eaten either, and I will accept your kind offer but I am most curious about your asking about the sewing."

"I have a place of business in America that sells dress goods and have been thinking that I might hire someone to make dresses to sell in the store and to do some custom sewing when the need arose. What do you think?"

The food and tea arrived before she could answer. While they ate she thought about what he had said. "Not knowing anything about business in America, I hesitate to recommend anything. But I think the idea is good. Have you thought about whether you would pay an hourly wage or piecework?"

"I don't know; what do you suggest?"

"If there is plenty of work, then hourly is better for you and piecework for the seamstress. Unless she is a slow worker then it is better the other way around." They got busy then on their food and the talk dropped off. While eating, John was thinking, "This young woman is not just pretty but intelligent, too; and she has a nice figure under that cheap dress." She was thinking, "I like this man, not just for the way he thinks but he is tall and handsome and has money, too."

Now his mind started on a new thought, "How about if I ask her to come to America to work for me. That would bring in a whole new set of problems, when would pay start? Who pays for her passage over? We would have to have separate cabins. Or: if we were married it would be less complicated. Where did that come from?"

She said, "You look like you are thinking hard. Is there a problem?" For a few moments he didn't answer, then said, "I was thinking of asking if you would like to come to America and work for me and all the problems that that would entail came to mind."

"I can see that there would be some concerns for you. Don't you have seamstresses over there?"

"Yes, I guess that would be the smart way to go, but if you worked for me you could help me pick out material and so on to take back with me."

"I could still do that. You could hire me to help with the buying and even more important to take you to the best and cheapest places."

"How much in the way of wages do you want?" She thought for a moment then thinking of a high number replied, "How about ten shillings a week?"

"I'll pay you twenty." She was a little shocked; she had expected him to argue for a lower wage, not a higher one.

"I accept. When do we start?"

"Well, I sail in two weeks, so I would like to start right away. Have you anything pressing to keep you from starting right away?"

"No, my flower business is not pressing. Besides, I think it will be fun spending someone else's money. When would you like to start?"

"Well, how about in the morning? We can meet here for some tea and then you can help me spend some money."

"I am looking forward to it. I will see you in the morning then."

"I hope you won't think me rude but as a representative of my company you will need to look the part. Do you have some nice clothes? If not it would be my pleasure to take you shopping this afternoon to acquire some. I know that that sounds very forward of me, but I am just trying to help if you will permit it."

"A gentleman just doesn't buy a lady clothes when they have just met but being from America you may not know any better."

"If you are going to work for me, we should have enough of a working relationship that you will overlook a little of what you consider bad manners so that we can get the job done. Plus I find it hard to believe that a woman would turn down a free shopping trip." She smiled.

"I just want it understood that I am a good girl and it has to stay just for business."

"I agree." Leaving the inn, she took him from shop to shop to buy her a full outfit from head to foot. John began to see as she tried on different outfits that he was more than just a little attracted to this girl. At the end of the day John suggested that she should put it on and that they should go to dinner. "All right, but I will need to bathe and wash my hair before I put on all of these new things, so it will take me a while."

"Right, I will send you home in a cab and you can tell the cab driver what time to pick you up and then meet me at my inn." She was hesitant but John wouldn't take no for an answer. So a time was agreed upon to meet. John hailed a cab and they parted. He thought that a bath sounded like a good idea; he went back to the inn and got ready for the evening. Knowing what Margaret was going to wear, he put on business clothe: white stockings, white pants, blue weskit, dark blue jacket, white shirt with a ruffled front. He combed his hair, which he wore cut short. He looked in the mirror and said to himself, "I look good enough to impress her. Now why did I think that? She is just going to work for me." He put it out of his mind and went down to the tap room to order dinner to be ready at the appointed time and in a small private dining room. He also wanted a good wine and good food.

At her room in a rundown house in a shabby neighborhood, Margaret was getting ready for her bath. She hauled hot water to an old tub in her room that she had borrowed from her landlady. As she undressed she started thinking about John. "He is a very nice man and handsome too. But it scares me to think of going to the colonies. Oh yeah; it is America now. I forget. I don't know how this is going to work out but I am afraid that I might fall in love with him. If he goes without me it will break my heart. Maybe I should try to keep this strictly business. I'm not even sure that that is possible. I am going to have to find a book on the Wild West and read up on it." She dressed very carefully and did her hair with care simply to keep it strictly business. Maybe by looking good she could make up for not being from a good family.

He sat at a table in the tap room where he could watch out the window for her cab so that he would be handy to pay for her cab. He ordered ale to drink while he waited; he didn't want to be drunk when she arrived. He was thinking about all of the different types of merchandise that he needed to buy and have packed in crates to ship home and arrange for the hauling to the ship. He had been thinking lately about opening a trading post out west to trade with the Indians and the fur trappers. That would take a whole different type of stock. And getting it out west was another shipping problem to contend with. Just then he heard a cab stop out front of the inn; he started for the door, then stopped. That wasn't her getting out of the cab. This lady was very classy and pretty. Then she turned and looked at the inn; it was she;

He ran out the door and ran to her and while paying the cab driver he said, "I'm sorry I didn't get here sooner, I didn't recognize you all dressed up, you look beautiful."

She blushed, "I had hoped that you would like it, you paid for it."

They went into the inn and the landlord showed them to the private dinning room. John helped her to be seated while the landlord served the wine John had ordered; he told him to bring the food. They started talking about all of the shopping that they had to do and John told her of his idea about a trading post out west. All of the time he is talking he is thinking how beautiful she looks in the new blue low cut dress. He was having a hard time keeping his eyes from the breasts showing at the top of that lovely dress. She acted like she didn't notice and kept her eyes on her food while thinking that he must really like this new dress, especially the top. She had never eaten in a private dining room; the food was spectacular. There was roast beef, some kind of fish, and chicken, too.

"John, the food is wonderful, and the wine is so light and good. Thank you for all of it. Tonight has been wonderful. I can't see how that my help in your buying is going to be worth all that this has cost. Are you so rich then?"

"I came to England because my father died. I have sold his business, his house and his horses and carriages and the rest, so I have enough."

"I am sorry that your father died. Were you close?"

"Not as close as I would have liked; he was not a man you could get close to. He kept everyone at arm's length. But I don't plan to waste his money. I will buy, or I should say we will buy all we can for two stores back home. It has to be packed for shipping and hauled to the ship so there is a lot to do."

They talked for a while longer, then he put her in a cab and gave her money for a cab in the morning and retired for the night. She said that she could walk back to the inn in the morning but he said the streets were full of garbage and horse droppings and they weren't safe for a beautiful woman alone. He didn't go to sleep right away.

His thoughts were too busy with her and the shopping to be done on the morrow. He was sure that if he didn't stop thinking about how she looked in that low cut dress he would never get to sleep.

In the morning John was seated at the table by the window when the cab pulled up and Margaret got down looking just as lovely in the daylight as she did in the candle light the night before. John stood as she came into the room; when she walked over to the table he told her, "Margaret, the merchants that we will be going to visit today are going to be so impressed with your beauty that they will lose money from being distracted."

"Thank you John. I think it is just the clothes that you bought, but thank you anyway. Did you notice that we have both been very forward in that we have both been calling each other by our first names right from the first?"

He thought, "The way things are going I won't need to know your last name except for the marriage certificate. Well, how did that get into my thoughts?" Out loud he said, "I am not sorry that we have become so familiar, but I don't know your last name."

"It's Shannon. A good Irish name."

"Well it's nice to meet you, Miss Shannon. I hope you will forgive me if I forget and call you Margaret now and then."

"Please do, I think it's too late to start now, don't you?"

So after a light breakfast they started on their buying trip. She took him first to several places where they sold fabric and other dress making things. After leaving she said, "John, you bought enough material to make a dress for everyone in London."

"I may not be back here for a number of years, and besides I will need enough to keep my future wife busy making dresses for my stores and for herself."

"So you have a fiancé waiting for you at home?"

"No, I have someone picked out here but I haven't asked her yet. Why, are you interested in applying for that job, too?"

She thought "I might but this is going way too fast." But she said, "Aren't you the bold one? We had better get on with our shopping before you start telling me how many children you want, too." They both laughed and moved on to more supply establishments. By the end of the day they had bought a lot, and arranged for the packing and shipping of it all.

At dinner that night Margaret remarked, "That was a very interesting day, John. Did you buy everything that you needed?"

"No, I need to buy supplies now for the trading posts out west. The stock there will be a lot different. I won't need much in the way of dress material but I will have some material for shirts. I will need trade guns, black powder, lead for bullets, bullet molds, traps and whiskey of course. And a lot of little things, too, like sewing needles and thread, fish hooks and fish line, buckets and axes, knives and so on." After dinner, he commented "I have never been to a show at a theater, have you?"

"Oh, I know of a great one. Let's go."

The next day started with an early breakfast; then they traveled from one place selling hardware to others with weapons and powder for sale and so on all day. This went on for three more days. At dinner at the end of this time, he said, "You know you have been indispensable to me for all my work here. How about going to America to work for me there? You don't have to answer me right this minute. The salary would be good. Although I can't promise good living quarters until the post is built I can promise some real adventure. Think of traveling with the wagons hauling all of that stuff that you bought across to the Ohio River then by steamboat down the Ohio, then the Mississippi, then up the Missouri all the way to the Yellowstone. It will be the greatest adventure you could ever imagine,"

"Oh, I can imagine all right; I can imagine hoping to stay alive among the wild savages, the great bears, lions and wolves and what becomes of me if something happens to you? I would probably be sold to the highest bidder for so many furs or horses. No, thank you. Now if you would pay me what you owe me."

He handed her a small bag of gold coins and then took from his pocket a wedding ring. "How about going as my wife?" All she could do was just stare for a long moment then slowly she opened the bag of money and seeing it was gold and not silver she was even more surprised. She sat back in her chair and looked at him for a full minute. "You still haven't said what happens to me if something happens to you or how many horses I am worth."

"I will make out a will leaving everything to you. I have no relations to contest it. You will be a rich widow."

"Well, you seem to have thought all this out. When did you decide to ask me?"

"I was sure that you are beautiful the first time I saw you, and after the second day of being around you I was sure that I was in love and that I wanted you for my wife. I was afraid you would think that I might be a little bit forward, but I haven't much time before my ship sails. And I need to go with my merchandise."

She was very thoughtful and sat looking down at her hands for a few minutes; still looking down, she said "I thought you might ask me to go with you to work for you, but it never entered my mind that you would ask me to marry you. You should marry some merchant's daughter not a flower girl. Since I met you I have been reading all that I could find on the wilds of America. It sounds very exciting but very scary, too. You don't even know what kind of family that I am from or if I can cook or if I snore or if I'm even a virgin."

"I don't care about any of that. You don't know if I snore either and I can hire a cook. In America we don't have a class system like you do here. Your only class is beautiful anyway." After a pause, "Do you need more time to consider it and keep me suffering without an answer?"

"No."

"No you won't marry me or no you won't make me suffer?

"Oh I will marry you but I'm sure I will make you suffer, too."

They got up from the table laughing; right there in the dining room at the inn he took her in his arms and kissed her. She took his arm and they went up to his room.

The wedding was small, she had few friends and no family. Only two friends of his father came. The preacher was a friend of his father and preached a good sermon from Ephesians on how a wife should submit herself to her husband and the husband should love his wife as Christ loved the church and died for it. The reception at the inn went well; the food was good. The wine was plentiful; a small band was there for the dancing. The honeymoon was spent shopping for the trip, and other more romantic things which will be left to the imagination of the reader.

CHAPTER TWO
THE VOYAGE

All was finally ready and loaded on the ship; the Captain gave the orders to heave the anchor and set the sails and the ship gathered way. John and his new wife watched the land slip by from the rail while holding hands.

"I have never been out of London before. This is very scary, you know?"

"Yes I know, but you are a courageous woman. And I know we are going to have a wonderful life together."

And so the adventure began.

The other passengers included two businessmen, and two families. They all ate dinner at night with the Captain in his cabin. Captain Wright was a big bearded man with a loud deep voice. He was a kind, friendly fellow who told entertaining stories. The first night at dinner the Captain got everybody to tell about themselves and because the Captain knew John, he told how he met his new wife and where they were going. One of the families, the Smiths, were going to America for a new start in life, hoping to someday get some land of their own and farm. They had no money to start on, so needed to get jobs to make a living in the meantime.

The other family were going home after a trip to visit family in England. The two men were going to sell their products to American stores. The first few days some of the folks were a little seasick but after that the dinners with the Captain were an enjoyable event. One night, when they were back in their cabin after dinner, Margaret said, "I like the Smith family, John, after getting to know them. I think it would be good to have them along on our trip. You said you would have to hire people to help build the post and to haul all the merchandise out there. He has worked as a carpenter, and she could help with the cooking for the crew building the fort. And the kids are such cute little rascals. I know it is your decision but I'm all for it."

John laughed.

"It is not proper for a wife to be bossing her husband around but I have been thinking of asking them. It would be a big load off their minds knowing they had jobs when they arrived. And I like them, too."

"Let's go talk to them now, okay?"

"Yes." And they went out.

The Smith's cabin was just next to theirs so they didn't have far to go. When they knocked Mr. Smith answered. "The cabin is small but I guess we can all crowd in."

"It looks like your children are asleep, so maybe we could go to our cabin. It is larger and there are only the two of us."

They went next door to their cabin. John sat on a trunk and his wife sat on the bed; the Smiths sat in the only chairs. After some small talk, Margaret asked John, Can I ask them? I'm too excited to wait for you to do it."

He laughed. "Go ahead. It was your idea anyway."

"You said you were thinking about it, too. Anyway, we thought that since you didn't have jobs when you get to America that maybe you would like to work for us. John said I should warn you that we plan to open a trading post in the west to trade with the Indians and the trappers for fur. It will be a long trip, although most of it will be by steamboat and that should be fairly comfortable. When we get to where we are going there will be a lot of work building a small fort and houses and furniture, etc. And you can help too, Mrs. Smith, with cooking for the crew doing the building and with the cleaning of the buildings. Well, I know that my husband should be doing the asking but that's the jobs. Any questions?"

"I have a few," said the husband. "What do we do when the building is done?"

"You can stay on and work in the store," said John, "or take the first boat back to the coast, or take up land and farm or raise livestock. You can decide that then."

Mrs. Smith said, "Will there be other folks there?"

"There will be a lot of trappers and a lot of them have wives. There will be others too, a blacksmith, horse traders, a carpenter shop. Even a gunsmith. Usually a town springs up around a trading post. Your husband could even run for mayor."

"It sounds like a great adventure to me," said Mr. Smith, "When do we start?"

"As soon as we land in Boston. What do you think, Mrs. Smith?"

"It is very nice of you to give us jobs. We were very worried about that. Are the Indians where we are going friendly?"

"Some are and if we don't cheat them in trade, the unfriendly ones won't attack us if we don't wander too far from the post. We will be very busy; we will plant a large vegetable garden and build a smoker for the game that we get. In fact, we will have to build the fort strong to keep the buffalo from knocking it down. They come through there in the millions. They weigh up to two thousand pounds. One can feed the whole town. The trappers will bring meat to trade, too. Now listen to me talk. I sound like I have been there. But all I know I learned from books. The experiences that we get out there will be better than any book. In fact I will keep a log of all we do."

That log told of a storm a few days later that made them all wonder if they hadn't made a mistake. All but the kids got seasick. It's hard to keep track of a couple of rambunctious little kids when you're not feeling too well. John finally took them to his room to play games.

When the lookout called *land ho* they all went on deck to watch. The Captain came over and said, "It will be the middle of the night before we drop anchor. Boston is a way down channel from here but you might enjoy watching the shipping that we pass and land that we go by on the way." He turned and yelled to the man at the wheel. "Starboard a point." After he looked at the sails and walked over and looked at the compass, he called out to the passengers in a loud voice, "I'll see you for a last supper at seven." Then he went below. Everyone stayed on deck to watch the New World sail by.

John stayed on deck after everyone else went to bed. He couldn't sleep anyway; he was too excited. As he watched, other ships passed heading out to sea. John thought of the hours he and Margaret had spent on the voyage getting to know each other. She said she was a little worried that on calm days they might be rocking the boat. He smiled to himself; she had a good sense of humor, that's for sure. And she had courage too. He didn't believe any other white women had gone up the

Missouri as of this date. Thinking about it now he couldn't imagine doing all this without her.

CHAPTER THREE
BOSTON

It was after midnight when they got in; the wind was wrong so a steam tug hooked on and pushed the ship up to the wharf. As the sailors were tying off, the Captain came over and said, "I think you should come below for a few moments, John. We won't start unloading your freight until your wagons are on the dock so we can offload right onto your wagons. But I think you should see the maps first." John and the Captain went to his cabin and the Captain took out the maps of the east coast to show John. "You see here from Boston to the Ohio is a long haul. But if you stay on board until we get to Baltimore it is about half as far to haul your freight. And you can purchase or hire wagons there cheaper. And I'm going there anyway. And it will take less time by ship than by land which I'm sure the women will like it."

"Thank you, sir; that will save a lot of time. I will go now and wake my store manager. That way he can have the wagons here early." As he went down the gangplank, John asked the mate if his wife awoke before he returned, to tell her that he would be right back. The lantern that he had with him did not put out a lot of light but it was good enough to get him to his manager's house without stepping in anything too offensive. John woke up his manager by tapping on his door with his cane. His manager, Mr. Park, came to the door in his nightshirt carrying a large pistol. On seeing that it was John he said, "Come in. Come in. I had no idea that you were in town."

"I just got in. The ship docked within the hour. We need to get wagons down on the dock by dawn if we want our merchandise to be unloaded right onto them. We will need at least two." Mr. Park was a little shocked. "Why so much? We haven't warehouse space for more than one big wagon load. Here, I'll put on some coffee while we talk." They went into the kitchen and while Mr. Park got the fire going and put on coffee, John told him of his plans for a trading post out west.

"We will have to haul to the Ohio River and contract with a river steamer to go west. By the way, you are getting a raise because you will have to handle all the freight coming and going in the future. I have set it up with merchants in London so that we can send an order for goods and they will ship it to you and you will ship what I need on to me. I will be shipping furs back for you to be used for payment for everything. I will also give you some shares of stock in the company so you won't feel you are doing all this work just for me. My father died while I was gone, and I sold everything in London. I am now your only boss."

"Well, I am sorry to hear that your father died, but I am happy to hear all the rest. Stocks and more pay will not hurt but I will need some extra help."

"You are now the manager of all the Boston business so you hire and fire anybody you see fit. While I was In London I got married. You will meet her today when you bring the wagons to the docks. Well, thanks for the coffee, you better get going to roust out the teamsters, and I need to get back to the ship and maybe get a little sleep before morning."

"I would like to wish you a hearty congratulations, Sir, on your marriage and you are right I need to get moving. I guess I have had all the sleep I'm going to get tonight."

John hurried back to the ship. On walking up the gangplank he handed the lantern to a man on watch and went to his cabin. Going in as quietly as he could so as not to awaken his wife he undressed and got into bed. It only seemed like he had slept a few minutes when his wife shook him awake saying, "Get up, lazy bones. The wagons are here, and a man on the dock is asking for you." He climbed from bed, got dressed and hurried on deck. Margaret was there talking to the Captain. She was dressed very nicely in one of her new dresses. The Smiths were there, too. He greeted them all and went to the rail and called for Mr. Park to come aboard. The sailor standing guard at the gangway heard him and let him pass. John led Mr. Park to the others; "Mr. Park, this is the Captain. Mr. Park is the business manager of everything east of the Mississippi and will be handling all freight going through here." They shook hands then John turned to his wife, "and this beautiful woman is my wife Margaret."

"Well it is very nice to meet you, Mrs. Brix. John didn't mention that along with the merchandise he was bringing back a wife."

"It is nice to meet you too, sir and it will be nice to see my husband's place of business, too." John then introduced the Smiths; "The Smiths will be going with us and working for us so you might see them from time to time. By the way, ladies, we will stay aboard ship, sail to Baltimore and land our cargo there. It is half as far to the Ohio from there. But you will have a little time here in Boston for some shopping. But don't miss the boat."

The Captain instructed them, "We will be unloading cargo all day, so I plan to leave on the morning tide. That gives you all day to spend some of John's money and see the sights."

Mr. Parks went down the gang plank first and told the teamsters that no more wagons would be needed since only the Boston freight would be coming off here. He then went to find a carriage so that his boss and his party didn't have to walk all over town. He came back with a large carriage. They all got in. The little boys and Mr. Park rode up front with the driver.

They went first to the Brix Co. store, which at that time of day was open for business. The two clerks were busy with customers so they wandered around looking at everything. John said, "While we are here I want everyone to pick out some warm clothes for the trip." Mr. Smith, whose first name was Mark, said "That is very kind of you, sir, but I'm rather short of cash."

"If you like we will keep track and take it out of your wages. But I would be happy to pay for them. The weather up the river will be below zero most of the winter, and you will need warm clothes. Besides it's cheaper to buy them here than there."

"Oh, Mark," Margaret interjected, "let John pay for the clothes. I'm sure he will have a lot of other things he will say you will need. Come on Lisa, we will let them argue while we pick out things for you and me and the children."

Mark and John got blanket coats, deerskin pants, good boots, heavy socks and long johns for themselves then went to look at weapons. They picked out four long rifles, cap and ball, four pistols and a knife each. They took powder horns, sacks of balls, boxes of caps, patches, cleaning gear, and satchels to carry the small things in. Margaret looked at the pile and laughingly said, "John, you have all of this on the ship."

"Yes, but it's all packed for shipping. I don't want to unpack the crates for just a few things and then have to repack them for the trip. Mr. Park, would you put all this in a trunk and send it down to the ship for us, please?"

"Yes, of course, and I am delighted to have met all of you."

After giving Mr. Park some final instructions they all got back into the carriage for a guided tour of the city. Stopping at his old place of residence, he told his landlord that a wagon would be coming for his things as he was off to the Wild West, leaving this very day.

After seeing the city sights and shopping for small things for the trip, they arrived back at the ship to find that John's furniture and everything they had purchased earlier were stowed and the ship ready to sail.

They all watched the steam tug tow the ship away from the dock and out into the bay. The sails were set, and they were on the way. They stayed on deck and watched Boston slowly slip away over the horizon then went to supper in the Captain's cabin. While they ate, Captain Wright advised them, "I took the liberty of keeping your guns and ammunitions out so you could practice with them on the way to Baltimore. I doubt if Mark here has ever fired a long rifle and you will need to learn. There are gangs of robbers on the roads to the Ohio and you don't want to have to learn under fire."

John said, "That sounds like a good idea; the women can learn to load for us, too." The women looked at each other with a rather surprised look but didn't say anything. The Captain said, "You will probably find other travelers in Baltimore who are headed that way and you could join them for safety's sake." The talk went on for a while but the kids were tired so Mrs. Smith took them to their cabin, put them to bed and went to bed herself.

In the morning after breakfast, all went on deck for rifle practice. First John showed them how to clean the guns. There was still some grease in the barrels from shipping. He then showed them how to load. After making sure the rifles were loaded right, he put a cap on one and handed it to Mark. He signaled to a sailor up forward in the bow to throw a bottle out. He told Mark to sight in on the bottle and squeeze the trigger. He missed. They kept at it with the women loading for two hours. They then cleaned the guns and went to clean the powder off themselves. They practiced every day until Mark did better shooting and the women got faster loading. In a few days they sailed around Cape Charles into Chesapeake Bay. Two days later they dropped anchor at Baltimore.

CHAPTER FOUR
BALTIMORE

The women were excited about this great new adventure and chattered about what to wear and what to put on the kids. John left the ship as soon as a boat was lowered over the side; the Captain went too. He had to arrange dock space or they would have to unload into lighters, small boats, and that would be handling the cargo twice. John needed to arrange for wagons so headed for the wagon yard the Captain had told him about. He walked over to some men standing around there. "I'm needing to hire some men and wagons to haul some freight to the Ohio. Who do I see?"

An older man in buckskins looked him up and down and asked, "Why would a man in fancy clothes want to go to the Ohio?" The other men kind of gathered around as if expecting something to happen but just then a big fellow came from the office and yelled, "Hey. You men leave the man alone. I haven't got so many customers that I can afford for you to run some off. Now git." He turned to John, "Come into my office. Don't pay any attention to that lot. They just hang around here to get a job now and then. Now what can I do for you?" John reached out to shake hands; "I'm John Brix of Brix and Company, and I need to engage a freight outfit to haul to the Ohio and back. We are opening a trading post up on the Yellowstone and will be shipping merchandise in both directions." The big man, shaking John's hand said, "My name is Johnson and I'm glad to meet you Mr. Brix. How many wagons will you need?"

"I would like to buy one with four good horses that can be ridden when we get there. Then hire two more. I hear there might be trouble on the way so I would like to hook up with others who might be going over when we are. Can you advise me on that?"

"There is no problem with any of that. There are a couple of wagons heading out in a few days and a number of trappers heading back to the mountains. They will be happy to have you along. How many in your party?"

"There are two families, one with two kids. I would like to buy a good riding horse too."

"There is a horse and slave auction going on after lunch today, about three blocks up the street. It is a bit of a surprise to me that you are taking women and kids to the mountains. You and the other gentleman may have to fight to keep them. Those robbers on the trail to the Ohio would kill you just for the women. Be on the lookout."

John thanked Mr. Johnson for his warning, paid him for the wagons, and told him to have them on the dock after lunch so that the freight could be loaded right onto the wagons. As he walked up the street to the auction yard, he thought about the dangers that lay ahead of them and wondered if what he was doing was smart.

When he arrived at the yard he found that the slaves were to go first and the horses after. They brought out twenty bucks first. Since slavery was illegal in England John was not interested in buying anyone. The weather being rather cold he was surprised that the Negroes were just dressed in rags and no shoes. No one wanted to bid on one of the men. He heard a man standing near him say that this one caused too much trouble. When the auctioneer called out $100 John raised his hand. "Sold."

John went to the clerk and paid for the man. He then walked back to where he had been standing and the Negro followed him. John asked him his name. Sir, my name is Arco but the white men calls me Adam. Sir, my wife is going to be sold in the next group. If you would buys her too, I would be the best nigger you ever saw, sir." John thought about it for a minute.

"Arco, I am from England and slavery is not legal there. I hear it is not legal here to set you free but I plan to anyway." The Negro started to say something but John cut him off. "All right, I'll buy your wife. But I warn you we are headed west to the mountains and you could get scalped by the Indians. They may like your kinky hair hanging from their lodge pole."

"Sir, I am from a warrior tribe and not afraid to fight."

"Can you shoot a gun?"

"No, sir, but I can learn."

After the men were all sold, they brought out six women. They too had on just rags, and only two had shoes. One was starting to show that she was pregnant. John looked at Arco and he lowered his eyes and indicated the pregnant one. John didn't say anything but when she came up for bid he paid $300 for her. When the horses came up he bought a long legged grey that looked like it could run forever. Then he bought a big mule for the Negroes to ride. They rode to a Negro neighborhood where he bought them both some warm clothing and moccasins and took them to a bathhouse for blacks and had them bathe before putting on the new clothes.

At the dock the wagon master, Mr. Johnson, met them. "That ship captain is well organized. It looks like the wagons will all be loaded in another hour and you will be ready to go. What about food and tents and camp gear. Do you have all of that?"

"No, I was going to buy that here. Can you direct me to the best place?"

"Sure, the prices are pretty much the same all over town but I can get you a better price at my brother's place." John told the Negroes to wait while he rode to the ship and sent for his wife. When she came on deck he told her they had to go buy food and camping gear and for her to climb up behind him so that she didn't have to wade through the refuse on the streets to go with him. She thought that it was kind of romantic to ride behind him holding tight to his back. As they went along following Mr. Johnson, she noticed the two Negroes on the big mule following them.

"What has John done now?" she thought. He and Mr. Johnson were discussing the city and she didn't want to interrupt, so she waited until they got to the store before she asked about it. John, knowing she would be against owning slaves, said, "Oh, they were looking for work so I hired them to go with us to the West." She wasn't sure she believed him, but she didn't say anything, and followed him into the store to buy the things that they would need on the trip west. When it was all ready to go Mr. Johnson looked it over. "It looks like you got everything you might need but you will need another wagon to haul it in. I have a light one that that big mule could pull. I'll let you have it cheap."

"Yeah, I'll bet." John said laughing. He went out and told Arco to follow Mr. Johnson to the wagon yard and pick up the light wagon then come back to the store and load up all this gear and drive to the dock where they had been earlier. He then looked at Arco and said, "I'm trusting you Arco." He then turned to Mr. Johnson and said, "Don't let those men of yours give these people a bad time. If they do I will bring my men and come shooting."

He laughed. "Don't worry; they will be Sunday school boys. I give my word."

When Mr. Johnson and the Negroes arrived at the wagon yard there was only the big man in buckskins there. Johnson said, "I thought I told you to get." Bear Claw Jones said, "I plan to go to the mountains too but I'm broke. I need to hook up with an outfit so I can eat on the way out there." While Mr. Johnson fitted harness to the mule, Mr. Jones went on. "You know I'm a good trapper and mountain man but I spent all my money staying here this winter. I ain't et in two days." Mr. Johnson led the mule to a small wagon beside the barn. He and Arco hitched it up while Bear Claw kept talking. "If you would send a note to that fancy Dan telling him what a great fellow I am, he would be glad to have me along."

Arco looked the wagon over then helped his wife up onto the seat and climbed up beside her. Mr. Johnson had been thinking about what Jones was saying; he told Arco to have a good trip, went to the office and wrote John a note. He handed it to Jones. "Take this to Mr. Brix at the docks but I'm warning you if you give him any trouble on the trip out there you had better not come back here because I'll hear about it and I will stomp you down so small a cat will think you're a mouse and eat you."

Bear Claw, knowing old Johnson was as mean as he talked, picked up his pack and rifle and headed for the dock. He didn't know what ship to look for but recognized the teamsters old Johnson had sent and went over to them. He put down his pack. It was huge for it had everything he owned in it. He asked a teamster where Mr. Brix was and was told, "I don't think the boss will want to talk to you after you called him fancy pants this morning. What do you want anyway?"

"I don't have to answer to no mule skinner. Mind your own affairs and stay out of mine."

John, coming on deck, saw that the seamen at the rail were watching something amusing on the dock; he went to see what it was. He saw the tall man in buckskins put down his rifle and the teamster slip out of his jacket. He went down the gang plank, walked between the circling men and told the teamster to get his load tied down. Then, turning to Jones he said, "What do you want?" Jones just handed him the note from Johnson and watched as John read it. John, who was now dressed in buckskins himself, said, "Mr. Johnson seems to think that I might need you to reach the Ohio. Are you sure you want to travel with women and kids and a fancy pants all that way?"

"I don't know what that note says. I can't read, but I ain't et in two days and if I don't hook up with some outfit going west I'll starve before I can shoot some game to feed myself. You don't have to pay me. I will scout and hunt, and work just for grub."

"And start fights and make trouble."

"No sir, I will stay out of trouble."

John glared at him for a few minutes. "We don't have any extra horses so you will have to ride with your teamster friend. Throw your pack on his wagon. And no trouble."

They said their goodbyes to the ship captain and crew; with the Smiths and Margaret in one wagon and the others following, they headed up the street toward the camp of the others leaving for the west. John riding his big grey led the way with the Negros in the light wagon coming last. Arco and his wife, whose name was Ella, were very happy. Ella exulted, "It is hard to believe that the good Lord has sent us to a nice white family that ain't going to whip us or sell us away from each other. We needs to pray and thank Him."

She bowed her head and prayed out loud so Arco could listen. "Dear Lord of all people, we thank you for giving us such a nice master and we don't want to ask too much, but we are going into the valley of death and we ask for your protection please. I know you don't expect to hear anything like this from me, Lord, but will you help our white folk, too? In Jesus' name we pray. Amen." Arco mumbled amen too but Ella said, "Don't you think I said a good enough prayer for you to say a good amen to it?"

"We don't know how good these white folks are going to be to us yet. We only been with them one day."

"He said he was going to set us free once we were out of the slave states. How much do you want from a white man?" He didn't answer.

In a little while they drove into the camp of the people who were headed west. There were three wagons there, and a half dozen trappers. It looked good.

CHAPTER FIVE
TO THE OHIO RIVER

As they drove into camp a tall thin man walked out to meet them. John rode up to him, "Hello, I am glad to see that you haven't left yet. My name is John Brix, and we would like to travel with you." The man reached up and shook John's hand, "Name is Mariha Samson. We will be glad to have you along. We waited for you. We heard you were coming. The road ahead has a lot of robbers and we will need all the guns we can get." Mr. Samson told John where to park his wagons and asked if they would be ready to pull out in the morning. John assured him that they would be ready then asked about the road ahead. As they talked John's men parked the wagons and unhitched and picketed the teams, then set up camp while the women started cooking. Bear Claw helped with the teams then strolled over to where the other trappers stood around to say howdy. A trapper who went by Coonskin asked, "We saw you ride in on that wagon. Where's your horse at?"

"It was a long winter. If I still had it I'd eat it. I ain't et in two days." "Those folks you're with got plenty a food?" asked another camper.

"Yeah, we are going to eat good on the way out. Them women can cook. And they brought stuff to make pies and cookies and I'm with them and get to eat it all." A trapper by the name of Skinny Wilson said, "And we being good friends, you will want to share with us, right?" They all laughed. Bear Claw headed for the cooking fire. At the fire Lisa Smith told him to go round up some fire wood. We will need a lot for the night. He started to tell her to send the black man, but smelled the food cooking and grabbed an axe and went. A women hadn't told him what to do since he was a kid but he figured the cooking would make him get used to it real quick, and like it. Arco also went after wood. Ella was making some kind of soup at her own fire. When Jones got back with wood the smell of that soup made his stomach growl like an angry grizzly. He dumped his wood and went a little closer to Ella's fire and just inhaled. She looked up. "It will be ready in about ten minutes, time enough to wash up before you eat." He thought "Man, this negro girl had better learn not to talk to me like that." Then he got another whiff of that soup and headed for the creek to wash. After two helpings of beans cooked with big chunks of ham, and Ella's soup and fresh biscuits and six cups of coffee, old Bear Claw felt almost human and looked better too with a clean face and all.

After dinner, while the men smoked and the women cleaned up, the other trappers and teamsters came over and stood around talking. Skinny asked John, "Can I come join your outfit? The smell that came over to us was the best I ever smelled." Everyone laughed. John said, "That was good, Ella. If these fellows give you the wherewithal would you mind cooking for them too?" Ella looked down at the ground, "You are my master, sir. I do whatever you say, sir."

"You don't have to Ella. It would be a lot of extra work. I'm sure though that they would be glad to help with just about anything you say, like chopping wood, cleaning the dishes or even washing their hands if you would cook for them." The men looked a little uncomfortable, but everyone else laughed and Skinny said, "I'd even take a bath once in a while for that kind of cooking." Ella smiled at that. "If you wants me to, sir, I don't mind." John stood and, looking rather mean, said, "If she or Arco have any trouble from any of you, all of you will be doing your own cooking. Are we clear on that?" The men all agreed and Mrs. Smith passed around muffins that she had made. The talk went to the road ahead. The children were chasing two fluffy white puppies around camp that John had acquired while in town. Later, when the women were through cleaning up after dinner, and the children were put to bed with their puppies, and the horses and mules were brought in close, John asked, Mr. Samson do you plan to have guards tonight?"

"Yes but I think that this close to town one should be enough. The trappers can arrange that for themselves. They usually sleep with one eye open anyway."

As they broke up for the night John told his men that they would stand their own watch and set it up with Bear Claw Jones taking the last watch. John had heard that most attacks came at dawn. The old trapper was the best man to have on watch at that time. Before dawn, everyone was moving, getting breakfast, hitching the teams, and breaking camp. When the camp gear was all loaded, Samson started them moving. Two of the trappers went ahead on foot as silent as ghosts, to scout for trouble. Next came two more on horseback to back them up then John and Samson, then the wagons; two more trappers rode as a rear guard. Everyone was happy to be on their way. John's people were excited about a new adventure; they couldn't stop talking about it.

Little Tom Smith was too excited to ride; he jumped down and walked alongside his dad's wagon, carrying a trade gun that John had given him. He was ten years old now so John believed he should have his own gun. As he walked he dreamed about fighting robbers and pirates and Indians and being a real hero. When he started falling behind, his dad yelled at him not to get lost and to stay where he could see him.

They stopped at noon to have lunch and rest the horses and mules. After lunch, with the trappers talking about the good food, they headed west again. It was early spring and darkness still came early so they stopped in a clearing big enough to circle the wagons before it got too dark to gather fire wood and water and picket the animals. John told Valines and Perkins to hide out on guard. When they objected he told them they would be relieved as soon as a couple more men had eaten. John walked down their back trail a ways to see if they were followed. After he had watched from some bushes for a few minutes he heard a whisper of sound behind him and swung around with a pistol in each hand. It was Bear Claw. "Whoa now, you are sure quick with those guns."

"I was just checking to make sure you were all right. Just checking our back trail. How is dinner coming along?"

"They ain't ready yet, but vittles those women can put together, why the word will spread and you will have every trapper in the mountains trading at your post just to taste some of their cooking." They had been walking back while they were talking quietly. Suddenly Bear Claw grabbed John's arm and froze, staring ahead at the brush near camp. He gave a bird call and all the trappers grabbed their rifles and faded into the woods around camp. John looked around; Bear Claw did too. He decided to just walk back into camp like nothing was wrong. He walked to the wagon and picked up his rifle and noticed the teamsters had armed themselves and stood ready for trouble. The women paid no attention to what the men were up to but went on making dinner. Ella sent Arco to get water; as he went to the creek he saw one of the trappers sneaking through, silent like a ghost. He acted like he didn't see anything but hurried back to the wagons. Arco put down the bucket near the fire and went to the wagon and got two pistols out and put them into his belt.

When Margaret called that the food was ready the trappers started straggling in. When Bear Claw came in his shirt was wet. He went right over to John and said in a low voice, "There were two of them, spies for the robbers I think. We couldn't get them to talk. They won't be talking to the robbers either though."

"Did you bury them?"

"Hell no. The wolves and the buzzards got to eat too." He turned and walked to the fire to receive his plate full of food and a cup of coffee. John smiled and said to himself, "I guess you have to be hard to survive out here."

It was midafternoon the next day when they came on some burned out wagons with bodies scattered around. Skinny said it was about a month old. There was not much flesh left on the bodies but they buried what was left and moved on with all the trappers scouting ahead. Everybody had the feeling that if the two robber scouts had not been discovered, that they would have met the same fate as the other wagons. That night, when they made camp, John met with Mr. Samson and arranged for all the men to take turns standing guard. Three men at a time starting after supper. Jack Valines was the youngest trapper, he stood watch with John and Samson. Samson had been hauling freight over this trail a long time and still had his hair so he was trusted. He told John that there were more than twenty men in that robber band. They would be outnumbered two to one.

They kept watch day and night without any trouble for four days. On the fifth day, while they were stopped for the noon meal, a man rode out of the woods on a big black horse. He stopped fifty feet from the fire and looked around. Mr. Samson walked out to meet him; "Well, what can we do for you, Sam? Would you like some coffee before we shoot you or maybe some lunch?" The man looked surprised, then said, "Well if you know me, you know what I want. If you start walking back down the trail and leave the wagons and the women you won't be killed." A tomahawk came flying from somewhere and buried itself in the man's head. As the man fell, Mr. Samson grabbed his horse's bridle and ran behind a wagon with it as rifle fire started coming in from the woods on one side of the road. The teamsters and the women got down behind the wagons and started firing at smoke coming from the woods. The trappers slid into the woods on the other side of the road.

The firing kept up on both sides for a while. One of the teamsters went down and that left only eight guns on their side but with the women loading they were doing pretty well. Then Mark Smith got hit; that only left seven.

John was getting worried that they would be overrun when suddenly there was a lot of firing going on out in the woods. Three men burst through from cover into the road, looking back at the woods. John and the others shot them. After the first barrage of fire in the woods a lot of pistol fire went on then tapered off and the trappers started coming back to the wagons. Jim Perkins was the first one back. He said, "We circled around and took them from the rear. First with rifles then our pistols; we finished the wounded with our knives and axes. I don't think more than two got away. We will have plenty of horses for everyone to ride and some nice gear too.

The teamster that was hit had died. One of the trappers, Frenchy La Ville, had a bullet wound through his arm but it missed the bone. Mark Smith was hit with a through and through just beneath the left collar bone, no broken bones. He would be riding the wagon for a while with his wife driving. They buried the teamster, whose name was T.J. Polaski, alongside the trail. Valines, who was a good carver, put up a marker that read: T.J. Polaski who died fighting bandits and took twenty with him.

They moved on away from all the dead and made their night camp a few miles down the road. You would think that the mood around camp that night might be a bit solemn, but not true. The trappers were jubilant about their victory. The rest were relieved that they didn't have to worry about being attacked and could sleep safe at night.

The women fixed a wonderful meal that night. After dinner they sang songs around the camp fire. Arco and Ella, who had great voices, sang some old Negro spirituals and they all went to bed feeling good. But they stood their watches anyway. The rest of the trip to the Ohio was uneventful. That alone made everyone happy. They had their share of mishaps but no more bandits.

As they got close to the river John and Bear Claw Jones rode ahead to see what could be done about a boat. John wanted to get passage on a steam boat but a flat boat would do in a pinch. There were a few log cabins along the river which the residents called a town. The only two story building was the Wheeling Inn. Along the river there were two flat boats being built. But no steamboats. They rode to the inn and dismounted. Bear Claw said he would hold the horses and wait outside for John who, not saying anything, just walked into the inn. The main room was frontier décor with a plank bar set on two barrels, a couple of homemade tables with some chairs and some benches. The bartender was a big tough looking man with black hair combed back in a queue. He looked John over as he walked toward him and asked, "What can I do for you, sir?"

"I have some wagons coming along the road from Baltimore, and we are looking for passage down the river."

"Did you have much trouble? I hear the bandits have been bad this year."

"We saw some burned out wagons and dead bodies along the way, but pretty near wiped out the bastards when they attacked us. We killed twenty of them. Only two got away."

The man looked happy. "That should make it safe for a while. Wow, twenty, who did you have with you, the Army?"

John laughed. "No, just some good fighting men, seven trappers and six others with rifles and the women were loading for us."

"You brought women over that road? And plan to take them to the mountains?"

"Yes and kids too."

"I'll be dammed. I never thought I'd see the day."

"Are there any steamboats scheduled to land here in the near future, or do we have to go by flatboat?"

"There should be one in soon but he only goes as far as St. Louis. There is a small one that's in a yard up the river for repairs. He should be here in a week or so. That boat has been up the Missouri a couple of times, but the owner doesn't know if he wants to do it again. That's a tough trip."

"Well, how far up the river is it to where that yard is?"

"About a two hour ride I hear; I never been there."

"Well, thank you for the information. Would you tell my people when they get here to set up camp and wait for me please?"

John went outside and jumped on his horse and told Bear Claw what was going on as they headed up the river trail. While they rode John asked why Bear Claw didn't want to go into the inn. He admitted, "The last time I was there I got drunk and started a fight. That barkeep is an unforgiving cuss and probably would have throwed me out again." John chuckled and listened to all of Bear Claws difficulties from the last trip to the mountains while they rode.

It was getting on toward sundown when they rode into sight of the yard where the steamboat was being worked on. They rode to a building by a pier, dismounted and walked in. A thin old man was sitting behind a desk smoking a pipe. He looked up from some papers. "Well, Bear Claw Jones. I heard you had gone under. It's good to see you unless you're a ghost."

"No. I made it through another winter. This here is my boss, Mr. John Brix, He is looking for a ride on your boat." The old man got up and shook hands with John. "I'm Carl Idaho, but I am not going up the Missouri any more. Too much trouble. In fact, I would like to sell it. If you have three thousand bucks you can have it. I would really like to quit."

"You've got a deal." He pulled out a money belt from under his shirt and counted out three thousand dollars. They shook hands.

Bear Claw said, "If I had known you had that much money, well. . ."

CHAPTER SIX
THE BOAT

After Mr. Idaho put the money in the safe and locked the door they walked down to where they were working on the boat. On the way, John asked Bear Claw, "Did you mean that if you knew how much money I had on me you would have robbed me yourself?"

"I sure as hell would have tried. You can sure bet your ass on that."

Mr. Idaho chuckled. "I've known him a long time, and I never knew him to steal except horses from Indians."

John asked, "Now that I have bought the boat, what's wrong with it?"

"We had a couple of fights on the last trip. The repairs are patch and paint, mostly, and clean off the blood stains. Nothing serious. You'll want to talk to the Captain; he knows all the details." As they walked up the gang plank Mr. Idaho yelled for the workers to knock off for the day. Then yelled for all hands to the Captain's cabin. They climbed the stairs to the second deck and walked around the narrow outside walk and entered the captain's cabin. The captain and the pilot were bent over the chart table discussing some navigation problem. They looked up as the three of them walked in. Mr. Idaho announced rather joyfully, "I sold the boat."

"For a second there I thought you might have sold it to Jones, and I was about to quit."

Bear Claw said, "You don't need to worry. I wouldn't give you a hundred bucks for this leaky old tub."

The pilot responded, "When did you ever have a hundred bucks?" All laughed and Mr. Idaho introduced the Captain and Pilot as Captain Small and Jim Brown, the Pilot. John asked of the Captain, "When will it be ready to sail?"

"In two days. We need to load wood and supplies and finish the repairs. I hope you have some money left for all that."

"How much will you need?"

"Oh. a couple of hundred will do for now. We will need more when we get to St. Louis. But we could pick up some freight at St. Louis and that should help defray the cost."

"We have four wagon loads of merchandise and a dozen horses to haul. Will we have room for more?"

"That is quite a bit. How many people?" John turned to Bear Claw and asked, "How many of the trappers will want a ride?"

"They will all want to ride, but I doubt if more that two have the money."

"We will put it on the books and they can pay in furs when they can." The Captain interjected, "You may never see them again. Let's show you the ship." John told Bear Claw to go take care of the horses and bring their gear on board. Mr. Idaho was heading back to his office and told John that if he had any more questions to stop by after seeing the ship and he would be glad to answer them.

The pilot took John all through the ship, introducing him to the crew. It consisted of two deckhands, a steward, an engineer and a stoker. The steward also did the cooking for the crew. The boat was not a long one, about eighty feet on the lower deck not counting the paddle wheel at the stern. It had a twenty four foot beam. On the lower deck the front deck was open for deck cargo and horses. Next came the Salon where everyone ate and sat and talked between meals. After that the galley, then the engine room. On the top deck the wheel house was forward and raised four feet above the deck so that the pilot could see all around. There was glass in all the windows with shutters that could be raised when under attack. Next came the Captain's cabin and then down both sides of the ship were small cabins for passengers. John picked out one with a double bed for his wife and himself. The cabins were small. Most had bunk beds and a stand with a wash basin and a small closet and nothing else. After John had finished his tour and asked a lot of questions he left the ship and walked up to the office. When he walked in and sat down, Mr. Idaho asked, "Well, what did you think of her?"

"I like her. I need to know how much to pay the crew, and what do I do with her after we get where we are going?"

"If you give the Captain some operating money, he will make trips between the Yellowstone and St. Louis until the river freezes over in the winter then run freight on the Mississippi until the spring thaw. You can trust him. He has been doing those runs for a long time. And he will at least make enough to pay expenses and a little more." Just then Bear Claw came in; he broke in with, "What cabin do you want your gear in?"

"Ask the steward but don't put my saddle in there. Stow it somewhere else. And picket the horses. We won't load them until we are ready to sail."

"Aye aye, sir. You are already sounding like an old sea dog," Bear Claw says as he goes out the door.

Mr. Idaho gave John the papers on the boat all signed over to him and more papers with maintenance reports and pay for the crew records. They talked for a while longer then shook hands and John went back to the ship. He went to see the Captain, giving him the ownership papers and a paper giving the Captain the right to act as his agent on things concerning the boat. He gave the Captain money for provisioning for the trip. They were discussing that when the steward came in and announced that dinner was ready.

As they ate, John told Bear Claw, "In the morning I want you to ride back to Wheeling and get everything ready to load on the boat. We should be there by noon and I don't want too many delays in loading. Tell my wife to buy enough food to last at least to St. Louis."

"Good. We'll have good cooking now."

John bought lumber to build stalls for the horses; as soon as they pulled away from the dock, he put the crew to work building them. He helped to make sure they were done when they reached Wheeling. John stood on the outside walk with one hand on the rail and watched as Wheeling came into view. He became a little excited when he could make out his wife among all the people on the dock waiting for the boat to tie up. The teamsters were trying to back the wagons onto the pier, but too many people were in the way. As the boat neared the dock the wheel stopped and started turning backward to stop the boat. The deckhands threw ropes to men on the pier as the boat slowed. The stern wheel churned faster and the boat stopped. The lines were pulled in and were tied;

the gangplank was put across to the dock. Frenchy helped Margaret cross the gangplank. John went down to the main deck to meet her. He took her in his arms and gave her a big hug. "Well, what do you think of her?"

"Did you buy it? Aren't you afraid you might run out of money?"

He smiled. "We have a lot of money. You didn't answer me. Do you like your new home?"

"New home?"

"Well, for the next few months anyway. Come on, I'll show you around."

"All right but you have a few bills around town to pay. I bought food for everyone and sheets for the beds, just ours and the Smiths."

The Captain and Pilot were out on the second deck; John introduced them to Margaret. The Captain said, "I am very happy to meet you,

Mrs. Brix; do you know you will be the first women to go up the river with us?"

"The trappers told us that but you know you can't believe anything they say. What a bunch of liars."

John broke in with, "I need to go to town and pay for the supplies she purchased. Would one of you show her to her cabin? I'll give her the grand tour later. Thank you."

The pilot said, "I'll be happy to, if you would come with me, ma'am." Bear Claw came up with Jim Perkins carrying her bags and packages and followed them to her cabin. When she saw the size of it, she said, "I won't need all of this. I will sort it out. Do you have room somewhere for some bags, Mr. Brown?"

"Yes, ma'am. When you are ready send someone for the steward; he will take care of it for you. I'm sorry the cabin is so small. But we are glad to have you along, and will try to make your trip as pleasant as we can."

"Thank you. I'm sure everything will be fine. I'm excited about going."

As John left the ship he told the trappers to go pick out their cabins then help with the loading. Jack Valines went with him to pay the bills; he had the list and knew where to go. On the way back to the boat they saw Ella running from two men. She saw them and stopped. The men grabbed her. John pulled two pistol from his belt. "She belongs to me. Take your hands off her." One of them pulled a knife from his belt and moved like he was going to cut her. John shot him in the left eye. Ella said, "They tried to take Arco; he told me to run and started to fight." They started for the boat. As they went by the other man Valines cut him across the cheek. "That is so that I will remember you as a thief." He spoke with a slight accent. He was Creole French.

As they approached the dock area on the run, they saw that Arco had grabbed a club from his wagon and was fighting a circle of five slave catchers who were trying to take him. Two others were down with cracked heads. The townspeople and trappers were standing around cheering them on. John shot a man who was behind Arco with a knife. He looked like he was going to stab Arco in the leg to slow him down. The shot got everybody's attention. The slave catchers pulled pistols from their belts and turned on John. He walked right up to them; "These people belong to me. Since you have tried to take them you are nothing but thieves. I would put you under arrest, but I don't think there is a jail here. Maybe I should just hang the lot of you now."

"Maybe you would play hell getting that done," said one of them as he raised his pistol. Valines shot him. Since the trappers and teamsters were all around them and all had rifles now leveled at them, the slave catchers put their pistols away. One said "Too many runaway slaves have gone west. We are authorized to take them and check their papers."

"Yes and tear up their papers and sell them again. Let me see your authorization papers. If they are in order I won't hang you." The locals all had big grins on their faces. They knew that these men were just the kind of men that John said they were but they had the papers so John let them go. He told two of the trappers to keep an eye on them and told the rest to help get the ship loaded. John went up to his cabin and found his wife a little upset.

"I just saw you shoot a man. I know that it saved Arco from getting stabbed but it is hard to believe that my loving husband is so hard."

"I'm afraid that I am going to have to be judge and executioner from here on out or there won't be any justice at all. Those men would have taken Arco and Ella from us if I hadn't stopped them. There is no law west of Baltimore. We have to make our own. How is the unpacking going?"

"I had to send the trunks to storage but look. There are sheets on the bed and curtains on the windows. I checked on the Smiths; they have two sets of bunk beds and the children are very excited about the whole thing. Mrs. Smith says all is well and that she and Ella are going to do the cooking. The pilot says that the steward is not a good cook. The dogs are in their cabin, too."

The Pilot blew the whistle and the Shannon backed out into midstream and started down the river. The Captain stopped by John at the rail. "It's four hundred and more miles as the crow flies to St. Louis but over six hundred by this winding river. From St. Louis to the Yellowstone is about the same. I hope you like your new home."

CHAPTER SEVEN
THE TRIP

The first few days, the Smiths and John and Margaret lined the rails watching the shore go by. They were overcome with the beautiful forest lands they passed through. Except for the time spent racing around the decks, the children were there, too. Ella did most of the cooking with help from Lisa and Bear Claw, who was needed to sample everything to make sure that the quality of the cooking was the best. Arco kept the fires going but spent a lot of time watching out of the windows, too.

When darkness came, the Shannon would tie up for the night and sometimes a trapper or two or three would go ashore and shoot a deer or two. That gave them a lot of fresh meat. And with the pies and cakes that Lisa Smith made the food was great. The days slid by without much to do. The trappers fed the horses and the mule. The crew kept busy running the boat. They passed a log raft or two and a couple of flatboats and another small steamboat headed up river but nothing very exciting. Most of the time now was spent in the salon. John had to tell the trappers to watch their language with the women and kids there. He made them leave their pistols and knives in a chest by the door so no one would get shot over a card game. Rifles and powder horns were in a rack nearby too. The Captain said that there would be need of them on the Missouri. John had purchased four swivel guns off of a ship to mount on his fort but now he and Mark Smith dug them out and with some help mounted one on each side of the boat. Captain Small wished he had had them on the last trip. They sailed on.

Cairo, at the mouth of the Ohio, was just a few cabins and stores and of course a couple of saloons. It marked a big milestone on their trip, so everyone went ashore. John gave each of the trappers two dollars so that they could get a drink at the saloons but not enough to get drunk and cause trouble. He went with Margaret and the Smiths to the stores to see what had come up the river from New Orleans, and to see what kind of prices they charged. They only stayed for a couple of hours. When the Pilot blew the boat whistle everyone headed back to the boat and they headed up the Mississippi. It was about a hundred miles to St. Louis from Cairo so they would be there the next day.

Darkness had fallen when the Shannon tied up to the wharf in St. Louis. John and Captain Small went ashore to buy the last supplies that would be available to them for the trip up the Missouri. While they were gone the crew got the small wagon ready to lower to the dock. They would need it to haul the supplies to the boat. Margaret wanted it to get herself and Lisa around town to do some shopping of their own.

When morning came the wagon was swung to the dock and the mule was led down the gangplank and hitched up. John decided that a couple of trappers should ride along so two horses were saddled and led down to the dock. Jack Valines and Jim Perkins decided they wanted to go so when all were ready, they headed for town.

The crew got busy cleaning the boat. Mark Smith and some trappers were playing poker in the salon. A large canoe came down the river and tied up alongside. One of the deckhands was yelling at the occupants to shove off. Mark Smith and Bear Claw went out on deck to see what was going on. One of the strangers called out, "Hey Bear Claw, I heard you had gone under."

"Not yet. What do you want?"

"We got a couple of Indian kids to sell for slaves. We only want fifty bucks for the pair. A right pretty girl and her brother."

"Get them up here on the deck where we can get a look at them." The girl stood up while the two trappers steadied the canoe. Mark reached down and lifted her onto the deck, then the boy. The girl looked to be about sixteen or so, and the boy maybe twelve.

Bear Claw studied them, "They are Blackfoot. We are headed right to their home country. If we took these two with us as slaves we would sure as hell get massacred."

Mark said, "I'll give you twenty dollars for them or blast you out of the water." With that he took out a twenty dollar gold piece from his pocket and tossed it to the trapper. At the same time he pulled a pistol from his belt and so did Bear Claw. The trappers shoved off and headed down stream. Mark turned to the girl, untied her hands and asked, "Can you speak English?"

"Some. They made me learn on the trip down here. Are you going to the Yellowstone country?"

"Yes and you are welcome to come along with us. But you are not slaves. You are free to go anytime you want."

"To go on the boat is better than to walk. We would be willing to work our way."

"I guess you could help the cook. She is a nice lady. You will like her." He took them down to the galley and introduced them to Ella. "Ella, these two want to work their way up the river. I said they could help you. Is that okay with you?" The kids looked a little scared; they had never seen a Negro before.

"Yes sir, can use some help with all these mouths to feed." She turned to the kids and asked, "Do you all speak English?" The girl, whose name was Dove, answered, "Yes, I speak more than my brother. I have heard of dark skinned people who are slaves to the hairy face. Are you a slave?"

"No, and the boss and his wife are the nicest white folk you could ever know. When you meet them you will see."

"You mean the white man that brought us down here was not the chief?"

"No, he works for the chief same as us. Now help me lift this big pot onto the fire."

With Frenchy driving the wagon and Coonskin and Perkins riding along, Margaret and

Lisa went around St. Louis buying what supplies were needed. Lisa said, "Prices are pretty high for being in a city."

"Yes, but this is the last place you can buy anything from here on west. All the furs are brought here from all the fur companies and shipped from here to England and beyond. So there is a lot of business done here. Here comes John."

By the time all of the supplies, the wagon, the mule, and the people were on board and ready to sail it was after dark. The Captain said they would sail in the morning, so they set the watches and ate dinner. Dove came in carrying a platter of steaks and her brother behind her with a platter of baked potatoes. John looked up with a questioning look.

Mark said, "While you were gone you bought these two kids from some trappers.

They wanted to work their way up river. I told them they could help in the kitchen."

Bear Claw added, "These are Blackfoot kids. Since we are headed for the Yellowstone, they may help us save our hair. That's their home country." He introduced John and Margaret to the kids.

John said, "We are glad to have you with us. After you have had dinner, the steward will show you to a cabin." They thanked him and returned to the galley. Margaret looked at Lisa and commented, "I don't think they were treated very well coming down the river. She looked like she was with child."

"Yes, she did, poor thing." Mark said, "Their hands were tied when they came aboard. If we meet those trappers again, we will read to them from the scriptures. You can lay to that."

As soon as it was light the Shannon pulled away from the dock and headed for the Missouri. This being only the second time for any steamboat to go up the Missouri, half of the population of St. Louis was there to see them off. The year before was the first time they had gone up the river, and they only made it as far as the Mandan villages on the Missouri. This time they planed to go all the way up the Yellowstone as far as they could go.

At first the brown muddy water of the Missouri ran alongside the green water of the Mississippi. Soon they could hear the turbulent river running bank full. When they turned west up the river there were whole trees coming down the river, and bodies of dead buffalo, brush, logs and all manner of floating stuff they had to navigate around. But even worse were the logs buried in the mud leaning downstream. If they hit one of those it would rip the bottom out of the boat and they would be on the bottom. John was glad that the Pilot was good at what he did.

Day by day they moved up the river. Many times they had to stop and clear a path for the boat to get through. Sometimes it was log jams, sometimes it was too many of the logs stuck in the mud. The boat would pull up to the obstacle, hook on. With the paddle churning furiously in reverse and the help of the strong current they would pull it loose. They passed Ft. Atkinson, the last military post, and moved through the twisty river maze. They stopped at some of the small posts along the river, and one Kansas Indian village to trade. Forts Randal, Recovery, Kiowa were passed. After rounding a big bend they saw Fort Pierre,

As they passed the villages just north of the Grand River, the Rees came out in force to attack the boat. Little Bear and Tom Smith were on deck with their trade guns; seeing the canoes come around the bend in the river, they opened fire. The Pilot gave the steam whistle three blasts and everyone came running, armed and ready. Two trappers on each side brought out the two swivel guns and put them into their mounts. As the canoes got close enough and started firing trade guns and arrows at the boat, the rifles started firing back. Then as the canoes kept coming, the swivel gun on that side fired. It shredded the two closest canoes and the warriors in them. The river channel was on the far side of the river from the village; as the boat moved close to that shore the warriors on that side started shooting. The trappers on the swivel gun on that side waited until they were as close as they were going to be, then fired. It was a little far but the effect was devastating. A lot were wounded and the rest fled. In the wheel house they had pulled up the window shutters at the first sighting of canoes. Now they lowered the front one.

It would not do to run up on a sand bar here or on a snag. They would all be dead. It looked like there were two hundred Rees in that attack. The Shannon churned on up the river past the Ree villages; though the canoes followed for a couple of miles, they did not attack again. The boys decided that they had each killed three Rees and that made them warriors. The men smiled at that. John made them clean their guns, under the supervision of Jack Valine who was so infatuated with Dove that he was becoming a pest to her brother. The women who had loaded for the men thought there were a lot of savages to fight off.

Jack Valines came to John and asked if he could buy Dove. He said,
"The women say that Dove is with child. I would like to be the father to the little one. The normal way with Indians is to buy a girl from her father, or

from her owner if she is a slave. Would you sell her to me?'

"She is a free person. You will have to get her consent, not mine. I think you should wait and talk to her father. It might help if you learn Blackfoot on the way."

Jack went down to the galley and asked Ella if he could talk to Dove alone. They went through the engine room and out on the lower deck to be alone. There was a lot of cargo stacked there. They stood leaning against it. Jack said, "I have heard you had a hard trip down the river, and you probably have no love for the white men, but I would like for you to be my wife. I love you."

"I am with child. I don't even know who the father is. My father would not like me being squaw to a white man."

"If I get your father's permission, would you do it?"

"If he doesn't kill you, and gives his permission, then yes." She gave him a quick kiss and ran back to the galley.

Five days after the fight with the Rees they reached the Mandan village. It was just north of another Ree village but they were not attacked again. They traded some with the Mandans, but not too much. They didn't want trouble with Tilton's fort just across the river. Mostly it was just a visit.

The Shannon stopped at Fort Berthold and traded for some firewood. A few days later, they reached the mouth of the Yellowstone and Fort Union. They stopped there to trade and get some information about the Yellowstone. They learned that there were three small forts near where the Bighorn ran into the Yellowstone. John told the trader that he planned to go as far as the boat could navigate before he stopped. The trader said he was sure to have trouble from the Blackfoot although that was Crow country.

Only the boat's crew stayed on board the Shannon while at Ft. Union. Everybody wanted to see the sights, and learn what life was like here. The women were a big hit. Most of the men here had not seen a white woman in a long time. Wherever they went they were followed by staring people, Indians of both sexes, and trappers. Mr. Smith and the boys and two of John's trappers kept close to make sure that nothing happened. John bought a bearskin coat that was big enough. He noticed a patched hole in it and asked if that was the bullet that killed the bear? The answer was that it was the one that killed the man that was wearing it. He liked it, so he kept it.

The next morning the Shannon headed up the Yellowstone. The navigation was just as bad as the Missouri. It kept the Pilot busy. In a few day's travel they reached the little forts by the mouth of the Big Horn River. Fort Sarpy was first. Then Henry's Fort and Fort Cass right across the river from each other.

The Shannon stopped and did a little trading at each one. But mostly John wanted news of the country. Each of the forts wanted to buy a keg of whiskey even though John doubled the price he paid for it.

CHAPTER EIGHT
THE FORT

Two of the trappers left them at Fort Cass to go spend some time at the Arapaho village to the south. The Shannon headed on up the river in the morning. By noon the next day they stopped. John and the trappers unloaded the horses and rode out, scouting for the best place to build their post. The place John picked was where another river came in from the south and curved westward to run parallel with the Yellowstone. It made a long finger of land that would be easier to defend. Some men went up the river to cut timber to build with. They made rafts and floated them down to the site where the fort would be built.

Everyone, even the crew of the Shannon, worked hard on the post. Except for the stoker. He had to keep the fire going in the boiler in case they needed to make a hasty retreat down the river. Some of the men went up the river and cut trees. Others dug a trench across from river to river to set the logs into up on end to make a wall.

Mark Smith set up a rack to saw lumber from logs with one man up on top and one down below cutting with a crosscut saw. As soon as he had some boards he started making furniture. A lot of tables and chairs and beds, and shelves for stock in the store. With so much going on nobody missed Little Bear and Jack Valines until Dove came to John and told him, "My brother and Jack have gone to ask my father if I can be Jack's wife."

"When did they go?"

"Three days ago."

"What do you think will happen?"

"I don't know, but you should expect some of our people coming to see what is happening here."

"Thank you for telling me. If you want to go to your people you are not a slave; you can leave any time you want."

She was quiet for a little, then looking up she said, "You have been good to my brother and me. I would like to stay if it's all right."

"You can stay as long as you like, you are more than welcome here."

The women were still doing the cooking on the boat but most of the men were eating on shore and camping out there in the open or in tents. The Crow Indians showed up before the Blackfoot. Some ten families crossed the river coming in from the south and set up camp. John went to talk to them with a couple of trappers who spoke their language. Through these men John learned that the Crows claimed all the land south of the Mussel Shell and that he should get permission from the head chief to build a fort there. He said he would send someone to get the chief's permission. John took the head man and his squaw aboard the Shannon and showed them some of the trade goods he had laid out on the tables in the salon. They talked through a translator. The man sent his squaw to get some furs and she brought back a large bundle. John inspected the furs and they did some trading. The Indian wanted a trade gun, a knife, some powder and shot, some red material for a shirt, and a mirror so he could see to put on his war paint. When they were done, John handed back about half of his furs. The Indian was surprised that John had not taken all his furs. The squaw took some beads and trinkets and handed John another pelt and headed out the door.

The word spread that John was an honest trader and he was busy for the next few days trading with the Crows. When they had finished with trading, the Crows packed up and left. One of the trappers that spoke Crow came to John. "I heard talk in the Crow camp that a party of Blackfoot are on the way. That is why they left in such a hurry."

"Did they say how far out they were?"

"No, but they must not be far away or the Crows wouldn't have been in such a hurry."

The fort was a long way from being finished, so John decided to defend the boat if there was an attack. He gave orders to hurry and finish the walls of the fort and for Mark Smith to stop building furniture and work on the ramparts on the walls. Two days later scouts reported that the Blackfoot would be there at dawn. John asked Captain Small to move the Shannon across the river to be ready to meet with the Indians.

At dawn about a dozen Indians came to the river bank and waited. John had the gangplank lowered and walked down to meet them. He didn't need a translator because Little Bear and Jack Valines were with them. Dove came out on the deck to watch but, when she saw who had come, she went down the ramp to join them. Her father and Little Bear got off their horses and walked up to her. Her father looked at her and asked, "Who did this to you?"

Little Bear said, "I told you what happened, father. Those men are not here. These white men saved us and brought us home."

The father asked, "And that young trapper says he wants to be your husband. Do you want this?"

"Yes father, and I would like to stay here at the fort with my husband. He has work here to do."

"Is he already your husband?"

"No father, I told him that he had to have your permission first." John was standing apart from Dove and her family, and a trapper was translating what was being said for him.

Dove's father signed for Jack to be brought to him and told Little Bear to free him and return his rifle and things then asked him, "How much you give for girl?" Dove translated and Jack answered, "One gun with powder and shot, one knife, and my horse." Dove translated again.

"Not enough," the old man said. John told Jack to bring his father-in-law on board and let him pick out some more stuff. Jack was a little worried that he may be working for John for a long time to pay for all that the old man wanted, but Lame Wolf didn't take that much. That night

Captain Small married Jack and Dove in the salon on the boat. After the Captain finished in English, Frenchy LaVille did the Blackfoot ceremony with Little Bear translating. The party afterwards was noisy with plenty of good food and drink.

While propped up on pillows in bed Margaret discussed with John, "I was told by one of the trappers that the Blackfoot don't let their girls marry white men. Why did old Lame Wolf allow it?"

"I don't know for sure, but I think it's because he loves his daughter, and she wanted it so much. Part of it is that the kids were sold into slavery and we brought them back to their people. Papa probably thinks he can get a lot more merchandise from his son-in-law in the future."

The Blackfoot people including Dove's daddy stayed around for a week, making everyone nervous. They had brought furs along to trade and

John was busy dickering for the whole time. During this time only about half of the men worked on the fort. The rest kept an eye on things.

Work resumed after the Blackfoot left. Dove hugged her mamma and papa goodbye and said goodbye to her friends who had come with them. Little Bear left with them, but told her he would be back for the fall hunt.

As soon as the walls of the fort were finished the cabins, store and stables went up. Hay was cut and stacked inside the fort, enough to feed the stock for the winter. A large smoke house was built and a couple of storage buildings built up on poles wrapped in tin to keep the critters out. John had even brought glass for the windows on the boat; these were the first cabins out there with glass in the windows.

When the cabins were done, and furniture and residents all moved in, they had a party. John sent a rider down to forts Henry and Cass to invite them to the party. Hunters brought in two buffalo, two elk, some deer and antelope. Most of it went in the smoker to save for winter.

The women were busy making bread, pies, cake, and cookies enough to feed an army. People arrived by canoe from Henry's fort and on horseback from Fort Cass. Tables were set up in the open space in the fort to handle all the people. Some barrels of beer were set up and some whiskey. To top off the drinks list, some bottles of wine came out, too. A whole young buffalo was turning on the spit. Also fish from the river, geese and ducks were all cooking. Some free trappers came by to trade, and were invited to stay for the feast. A couple of trappers got into a fight and John told them to wait until after they ate so everyone had time to watch. Some of the trappers helped get all set up to eat. Ella was heavy with child and Margaret told her not to help or lift anything, just sit. Ella said, "Negro women is used to working right up to the birthin'. I'm doing just fine."

"If you don't sit I'll ask Arco to sit on you and hold you down." Arco said, "I don't see no lap there to sit on, Miss Margaret."

John stood at the head of the long table and thanked God for a safe trip, the fort, the food, and asked that the new baby would be born healthy. Amen. The food disappeared quickly amid a lot of talk and laughter.

When the pies and cakes were gone and everyone sat around relaxing, John took Captain Small and Jim Brown, the Pilot, into the office, "I think you should head back down to Wheeling with what we have in the way of furs. If you make a decent run the wagons should be there to meet you. How many men do you think you will need for hunting and protection?"

"Five or six besides the crew would be good. With those swivel guns we should be fine. We do need to get going if we are to make it back before the river drops too much in the fall.

"Take the furs all the way, I'll give you enough money to operate on, so you wont have to sell them in St. Louis. I want them to go all the way to our factor in London to pay for next years supplies. I will give you a list of the supplies that I want to be sent with the furs. I'll have it ready by the time you're loaded. Tell Bear Claw to come see me, please, as you go out."

Bear Claw came in a few minutes later and sat down in a chair to wait while John finished writing his list. Without looking up John said, "I'll need some men to ride with the boat back to Wheeling and back. I will pay them wages to hunt and fight and load and unload under the Captain's orders. Good men, you choose."

Bear Claw, not looking too happy asked, "How many?"

Finishing his list, John answered, "I think five should do. I want to keep the best workers here to finish the building, and hunt to fill our storage buildings for the winter. So send the lazy ones. If all goes well they will be back in time for the fall trapping."

The Shannon left after loading all the fur and enough smoked meat to last them for the trip. She was to stop at all the forts along the way to offer to haul any freight and people down river.

That night when they were alone John asked Margaret, "How are the women and kids doing with their new homes?"

"We are all happy to be moved in. You need to get Mark to make cribs and high chairs for there will be four babies born to the fort before long." John stared at her for a moment. "Do you mean that you and Lisa are both pregnant?"

"Yes, Lisa thought she was too old, but on that long boat ride there was not a lot to do so they made good use of the nights. And you kept us pretty busy at night, too. I hope you will still think that I am pretty when I start to get big in the middle." John took her in his arms. "Don't you know that to a man women are the most beautiful when they are pregnant? Wow! Four babies! We will have to build a school before long if you girls keep it up."

"Well, build the fort bigger so that there will be room for them to play."

CHAPTER NINE
THE VISITORS

For a time things went routinely. Groups of Indians and sometimes free trappers would stop to trade. They usually stayed a few days and then moved on. John was in his office one day working on the books, when Bear Claw came in to report that a group of French trappers had arrived with an old priest. They had come a long way and would like to stay a few days to rest up before going home to Canada. John told Bear Claw to tell Lisa to prepare enough to feed the extra men then went out to meet the visitors. Jack Valines was talking to them when he arrived and introduced them.

Father Andrew *ici a la patron* John Brix. They shook hands; while Jack led them into the fort John told Arco to take care of their horses and to see that their packs were put into the bunk house. The old Priest carried a large flat deer skin pouch with him like it was worth his life if he lost it. John led them all into the mess hall for lunch. Frenchy La Ville came in and was introduced. He immediately told Father Andrew that all the people here were Protestants except for him and Jack, but would he bless the fort and baptize the new baby anyway? Amid a lot of chuckles Jack translated for those who didn't speak French. The old Priest still smiling at Frenchy's request, "I would be happy to. Do you mind if we eat first? It has been a while."

Lisa, Margaret and Dove were bringing in food; John stood and prayed a thanks for the food; Jack translated. Frenchy was asking a lot of questions while they ate; Jack was listening to the Priest's answers. John finally asked, "What's up?"

"They have been to Utah to study the cave drawings. Father Andrew made sketches; that's what's in the bag. He said he would show us after we eat." So when dinner was done, the good Father took his sketches from the bag and showed them to everyone. They showed a lot of drawing skill. The figures in the drawings were of buffalo and deer and Indians riding horses in the chase. But in two of the sketches the drawing looked like a blown up man with a big round bowl for a head. John asked the Priest, "What do you think this is?" The Priest answered and Jack translated, "He thinks it's a man from another world."

The old Priest told John through Jack to read Genesis 6 verse 2. John got out his old Bible and read a few verses, then asked, "Do you think this is referring to men from another planet?"

The old Priest, through Jack, said, "I believe that God, when creating man on this planet, did so on other planets either at the same time or before or after. That doesn't matter much. But the difference is that the devil is only here on this planet. This is his prison. So while we on this planet have spent thousands of years spending all our energies killing each other, the people from other planets have spent their energies on scientific advances. That is why they can travel between planets and we cannot do anything but create better weapons to kill with." When he finished talking and Jack had finished translating the room was silent. This was a totally new idea to all present, and they all had a lot of thoughts to ponder.

CHAPTER TEN
THE SIOUX

Life at the little fort went well for a few months. The gardens were growing well; a herd of buffalo came through and threatened to trample it all but the trappers mounted up and drove them off before much damage was done. The trappers added a few to the meat supply and dried the hides for trade. A week later two free trappers crossed the river from the south and brought the news that a large Sioux war party was headed their way. They had gotten the word from some Crow hunters they had met. John went out to meet them. "Did the Crow say how many Sioux we can expect?" The older man answered, "They said a big bunch which could mean fifty or more."

Two days later the sentry called down that some Indians were coming. John went out and ran up the stairs to the cat walk to see for himself. He saw that others were manning the cat walks too. Frenchy said, "They be Crow and they are in a big hurry. I think the Sioux are not far behind maybe so." John yelled, "Bring out the swivel guns and get them mounted and loaded. Get the horses in and leave the gate open for the Crows."

People were running everywhere. Some hauling water to the barrels on the cat walks for putting out fires. Some carrying rifles and ammo up. Everybody getting ready for battle and hoping not to have to fight it. John yelled for the long rifles to be ready to fire over the Crows at the Sioux if it looked like they might catch up to the Crows. John could see that the Crows were not a hunting party, but a few families riding two or three to a horse. They had abandoned all of their equipment and jumped on what horses they had and fled on seeing the Sioux. They raced their tired horses through the river to the south, across the open ground and through the gate. The men jumped off and ran with weapons in their hands, up the steps onto the cat walks ready to help defend the fort. The women and children stayed with the horses or went to the well for water. John thought, It's a good thing we dug that well. There must be a hundred Sioux out there and we would not be able to get to the river to water the stock until they left."

    The Sioux stopped out of range of the long rifles and looked like they were having a talk. After a few minutes a chief with a big war bonnet rode up close enough to yell up to the men on the walls. In English, "If you send out the Crow warriors we will leave your little fort alone." John yelled back, "We do not want to fight the Sioux but we will not send out the Crows either. Many Sioux warriors will die if you attack our little fort and we are well armed and ready."

The chief turned his horse and rode back through the river to the others. When they had talked it over they split up. About two thirds followed the river to the west so they could cross the river out of range of the fort. The rest waited until the others were in position before the chief gave the signal to attack. It was the hope of the chief that, while the warriors on the west were in charge, the rest could safely cross the river. John saw the plan and spread his men out accordingly. "Hold your fire until they are well within range. And you men on the swivels wait until they are in point blank range."

The chief gave the signal and the Sioux on the west screamed their war cries and charged. The Sioux on the south started across the river. The long rifles started to fire, then the trade guns. The Crows with no guns were shooting arrows. The thunder of the two swivels was almost together. The Sioux retreated. The long rifles kept firing until the Sioux were out of range.

There were almost two dozen dead and wounded Sioux around the fort and many horses too. John checked his men; only two had small wounds. The women had been loading during the fight. Now Lisa was taking care of the wounded. The Sioux came two more times to about the same effect. John now had three wounded bad enough that they couldn't fight any more and one of the Crow was dead. Then the Chief came across the river and asked if they could get their dead and wounded. John said to go ahead. He watched as many men came leading ponies pulling travois. It took them a while to pick up all the dead and wounded. It looked to be a lot of the Sioux were dead.

When the travois were all headed back to the west the Chief yelled up to John, "We go. You have fought well. It not worth so many men dying for a few Crow scalps." He turned his horse and rode across the river to the south and they all started leaving. Margaret came up onto the catwalk to watch the departing Indians. "While you were having so much fun killing Indians we women were delivering a baby. Dove has a healthy little boy. Come on down and see." Then she yelled, "Hey Jack, come see your new son."

John asked her as he walked down the stairs, "It won't be long before you will be having our baby too, will it?" She took his arm and as they walked down the stairs together she looked up at him, "No, but it's still a couple months off. Are you tired of looking at my fat figure."

"No, I'm beginning to like the look. How soon can we get you looking like this again?" She hit him. When they got to Dove and Jack's cabin they met Bear Claw coming out. He said, "Wait til you see Jack. He is holding the baby and goo-gooing at it like a silly girl." They went in to see Dove and the baby. John asked his name. "Well, we are going to name him after you."

"Oh. Handsome John?"

"No." Jack said. "John Brix Valines. We thought that if we name him with the name of a great man, he will grow up to be a great man too."

Margaret teased, "Well, it's a real honor to us, but if you want him to grow up a great man you should find someone else to name him after."

While the girls talked babies, Jack and John walked to the office. John wanted to write about the fight with the Sioux while it was fresh in his mind. One of the Crow men came in and asked if they could leave their women and kids there while the men went out and see if the Sioux left any of their stuff that they could salvage. John told them to go ahead and if they wanted they could take some trappers with them. He didn't think the Sioux would be back.

That evening at dinner Frenchy La Ville, being a little defensive of the old priest, asked John whether he believed what the old priest said about men from other planets. John replied, "Does anyone else care to know what I think?" Just about everybody said yes, so he went on, "Well, my father, through what he read, thought that when God created man on earth that He did the same on other planets. Now we believe that Adam and Eve were created to live forever. Then they sinned and began to die. But the devil is only here on earth, so we think that the people on other planets are not tempted to sin and so live forever. So if they build a ship to travel through to our planet, even if they travel at speeds that we can't understand, it would take years to get here. And yet we have the cave drawings. So we believe that they have been here, and maybe still are with us."

Frenchy said, "I think Skinny Wilson is one of them. But how did they get so smart?"

"We have spent all our time since Adam thinking up new ways to kill each other. They have been doing better things with their science. Look at the advances we have made in the last fifty years. If we had started six thousand years ago to advance in science instead of advancing in war, we would be as far along as they are now."

Coonskin said, "That's too much for my brain; it gives me a head ache." He got up and left along with a few others. John continued, "You might wonder why they don't make themselves known to us. God probably told them that they could go look at the animals but don't try to get friendly, because those animals bite. That's the same reason we don't try to pet the bears." Margaret queried, "Do you believe all that, John?"

"It's what my father believed. But it sounds reasonable to me. It doesn't make much difference to us anyway."

A sentry on the wall yelled down that a boat was coming up the river. John ran up the stairs to the catwalk to see if it was the Shannon. He would be glad and relieved to see that it had made a safe trip. By the time the boat had worked far enough up river to tell for sure if it was the Shannon the entire population of the fort was up on the catwalk to watch. When the Shannon tied to the wharf they were all there to celebrate. Margaret and John went right to the Captain's cabin to hear about the trip.

Captain Small reported, "It was a good trip but the river is dropping fast so we need to get unloaded fast and get down to St. Louis before it gets too low." John patted his back, "We are glad to see you."

CHAPTER ELEVEN
THE CAPTAIN'S STORY

They went right to book work and the log of the trip. The Captain reported, "We picked up a lot of freight at the forts on the way down, and brought a good load back for them. We also picked up a load of ammo for Fort Union and the Army. We also had a full load of passengers coming back. It was a profitable trip."

"You keep the extra money so if you run into some trouble downriver you will have enough to fix it. How did the trappers do for you?"

"They did fine. We had a little fuss with the Rees on the way back up the river but those two cannon made short work of that. The trappers want to stay for the winter trapping, but I could still use a couple of men for protection and hunting."

"I'll ask for volunteers. When the boat is unloaded and all the furs and hides are loaded you had better leave or you might have to carry it down the river. How are you doing for money?"

"I don't need any. How about you?" John laughed and he and Captain Small started going over the ship's books again. Margaret came in to inform them that Ella was going into labor, "So don't plan on getting much work out of Arco till it's done." Captain Small observed, "You are going to have enough kids around here to start calling this place Fort Nursery."

"Don't say that too loud, or these trappers will start calling it that. I guess we had better name this place before they do. How about Brixton, after the town in England by that name? It was named after one of my ancestors."

"It's your fort, I guess you can call it anything you want." Margaret went out and had a sign painted.

The Captain resumed his story of the upriver journey, "There was a lot of debris in the river this time, even more than before. We spent a lot of time getting through it. Even some of the passengers helped. We had some ammo for Fort Union and freight and mail for all the forts. We will have fur packs from all the posts going to St. Louis and some passengers wanting to get out before the river freezes up. We are doing pretty well as far as money goes. Some places want to pay in furs. I hope that's okay."

"Yes. Just put them in with ours for the Ohio. I have some letters to send too. I need Mr. Parks to send some soft material for baby blankets and clothes, which is one of the expenses of having all these women here. Trappers come here from all over just to eat some of their cooking and stare at white women. At least they do a little trading as an excuse to come so it pays. My wife even encourages the ladies to dress nice and do their hair to attract more of them." By the time John finished that little speech they were both laughing. They talked a bit longer, then the Captain picked up his books and headed for the boat.

CHAPTER TWELVE
THE WINTER

Once the Shannon was loaded with all the fur and hides, John had them load a lot of smoked buffalo and elk quarters to sell in St. Louis and other towns along the Ohio. The Captain said they would bring a good price.

John asked for volunteers to go with the boat but there were no takers. He knew that they would lose a whole years worth of furs by going so he added, "I know you would lose about one hundred dollars or so by missing the winter's trapping, so the two who would go will get their regular pay plus a hundred dollars bonus." Only one man raised his hand. "I know that you would probably not like to miss wading in the freezing streams and dodging the Indians all winter, but I need one more man." One man asked, "When do we get the bonus?"

"When you get to St. Louis. You can spend the winter there with Jim Perkin's girlfriend. And if you drink up the money you can borrow some more from the Captain when you see him against next year's wages." That did it. He had more than he needed. He told the Captain to choose his men. After that was done goodbyes were said and the Shannon sailed.

During all the bustle of the boat leaving Ella's baby was born. John and Margaret went to see them. The cabin door was open but John knocked anyway. Arco came to the door and, seeing who it was said, "It's your house and we're your slaves so I don't think you need to knock, sir."

"You are not slaves and here are the papers to prove it. It needs your full names to be legal. What is your last names anyway?"

"We don't got last names, sir. How about you name us?"`

John laughed but Margaret smiled and said, "How about Shannon? That was my last name before I married John."

"That would be a great honor but how about something short that maybe I can learn to spell."

John said, "How about Elk? That is easy to spell."

"If that be okay with you, sir?"

"It is just fine, Arco, but it is your decision, not mine. You are not a slave anymore. In fact you can apply for some government land and be a farmer if you like."

"Do you believe that that is really possible, sir?"

"Yes. Jack Valines, Mark Smith, and John Paterson and I are all applying for tracts of land. Mr. Parks, my Boston manager, is taking care of it. Now can we see that new baby, Mr. Arco Elk?"

A Crow scout rode in and said that there was a large herd of buffalo just south of them; he invited them to come join the hunt. John, Arco and four trappers rode out. John let Tom Smith ride along. He was eleven now and had a trade gun and knife and was very excited about the whole thing. They came up to some Crow hunters who had some squaws along to do the skinning. When they got to the herd, the men with rifles got down in the grass and started shooting. At first the herd didn't pay any attention, but after about ten of their number were down, they started running. The Crow took off after them. John had told Arco, or

Mr. Elk, to bring the wagon along after them to haul back the meat and hides. The trappers had brought some pack horses along too. They all went to skinning and cutting up the meat to haul back to the smoker. Two of the Crow squaws had stayed and were skinning two of the buffalo the Crow hunters had killed. When the wagon showed up the pack horses were already loaded and headed back. They loaded the rest on the wagon, then helped the Indian girls load their horses. John and Tom and the two squaws loaded what was left over on their riding horses and walked. It was a lot of meat. With a few elk and some deer it should be plenty for the winter. Tom and Arco would be busy smoking it all, and storing it in the store rooms.

John turned to young Tom, "Well, Tom, it looks like you are going to be busy with all the smoking to do. The gardens are doing pretty well; you will have to smoke some of that too."

"Yea, how much am I getting paid for all this work, Mr. Brix?"

"I'll have to check the books, but I think after you pay off the clothes that I bought you, and the trip up the river on the boat, and the rifle and knife, and the horse, at fifty cents a day, you should be in the clear in about three years. Give or take a year."

The next big event that got written in John's log was the birth of the first girl born at the fort. John went to see Lisa and Mark and exulted, "I'm sure glad someone had a girl. It is getting a bit crowded with baby boys around here. What are you going to name her?"

"We decided on Mary Louise, after Lisa's mom," Mark informed him. Lisa let John hold little Mary and said, "I think we should have a service this Sunday to christen all the babies. Do you have a service in your prayer book for that?"

"If I don't, I'll think up something; if we wait a week or two we can dedicate our baby, too." Sure enough in a few days Margaret went into labor. John, of course, was the typical new father. Pacing up and down and talking to himself about names. They had been so busy of late that they hadn't decided on any. Like usual the baby was finally born, and it was a boy. Dove and Lisa brought him out to show his papa and asked "Well, what's his name, Mr. Proud Father?"

"I will name him Charles Eugene after my grandfather. I'll call him Charley. How is his Mama?"

Dove reported, "For new Mama she did real good, baby come easy, and big baby too."

"Can I see her?"

"She sleep. You wait." When Dove let him in to see her she was nursing the baby; she looked very happy. "How soon can we make you fat again?"

"I'm kind of busy right now. Can you wait until he sleeps?" She smiled. John sat in a chair by the bed and watched his busy wife and thought, "This is now a new year, and we have a new year's baby and two other new babies. In a few months we will be here a year. A lot of free trappers have been trading with us. Men keep bringing in fresh meat. We are doing well. In fact very well."

"You look very serious, what are you thinking of?"

"I was just thinking that as long as the Shannon keeps running we will be doing fine if we don't get run over by some Indian tribe. I have been thinking of going to the Green River Rendezvous in the spring. We could get a message to Captain Small to go up the North Platte as far as he can; we can meet him there and pack the supplies to the Green River from there."

"This is you we are talking of. I hope it does not include me and Charley. How many men will be left here to guard the fort?"

"There will be Arco, and Jack. He won't want to leave his wife and baby. Then there are Mark and Tom and I'm sure we can talk some of the trappers into staying."

"The trappers are not going to want to miss Rendezvous."

"We will think of something; maybe if you offer to keep them in pies while we're gone we would have plenty of volunteers."

"How long will you be gone?"

"I think not over three weeks. I just want to get the trading done and get back."

"I don't think we have enough to make pies to last three weeks for more than two. Not the way these guys eat."

The snow was getting deep, but trade did not slow down. The fort being close to the mountains made it handy for the trappers to come sell their furs instead of hiding them until spring. Fort Brixton gave them more for their furs than they would get at Rendezvous. For one pelt at Rendezvous you only got one pint of whiskey but at Fort Brixton you got a gallon. Even the Blackfoot came to trade. Dove got to see Lame Wolf and her mom almost every month. They were happy about having a grandson and getting to see him often.

Little Bear rode in one day. He wanted to talk to John. John saw that he was real nervous when he was brought to the office. "It is good to see you, Little Bear. Have you come to visit or to trade?"

"I come to trade for some of my tribe. I would not do this but some of the warriors made me because I speak your language. They have captured a trapper and would trade him for four ponies."

"Is he here?"

"They have him across the river. I am to bring the ponies to them and he can come over then."

"Is he alive?"

"He is in good shape, but they took all his furs, horses and weapons."

John thought for a minute. He had some extra ponies that Indians had traded for goods and whiskey so he said, "Alright, would you go to the pony herd and pick out some that they will accept? Get some rope and halters from the stables. I will get a boat ready." John took up his rifle and possibles and headed for the landing. Frenchy and

Skinny Wilson were at the fort. John asked them to go along in case of trouble. With Arco and Skinny rowing the big boat and Little Bear holding the lead ropes to swim the ponies across the Yellowstone, they forded without too much trouble.

    Little Bear had left his pony on the north side so, leading the four ponies, he headed north into the trees to bring back the trapper. He was back in less than an hour leading a man in buckskins and moccasins whose hands were tied; there was a rope from his hands to the boy that was leading him. When they got to the shore Little Bear dismounted, cut the man's bonds and walked down to the boat. The trapper started talking fast in French. Frenchy said, "I know this piece of shit and he's not worth four ponies. Maybe one donkey. This is going to cost you, patron. He will want to be outfitted and all on credit. He's no good for nothing."

"Well, we couldn't leave him to be tortured by the Blackfoot."

All the way back across the river Frenchy was yelling at the French trapper. John understood some of it and it was pretty funny. As soon as they arrived back at the fort, John and the two Frenchmen went to the office so John could write it all down in the books. Frenchy said, "His name is Pierre Labough and he is my cousin, but don't tell anyone. He doesn't work or trap much. Just enough to keep himself in whiskey. He's not worth spit."

"Sounds as if you like him a lot. Maybe you would like to outfit him yourself?" Frenchy turned red in the face like he was about to explode, but John cut him off and turned to Pierre, "Do you speak English?"

"A little."

"So you know all the nice things your cousin said about you?"

"Yes, but I am willing to work for you to pay you back for rescuing me." John told Frenchy to take him out and put him to work with Arco on the saw mill.

John wrote in the log what had happened then deleted in the books the amount of loss from the horses. He started thinking about going to Rendezvous. Most of the trappers would go just for the fun of shooting contests, horse racing, gambling, and squaw chasing. Boys will be boys. Even though they got more for their pelts here, they would still go; they looked forward to seeing old friends and all the other things. He would send a message down river to tell Captain Small to meet him on the North Platte as far upriver as he could go. He would leave it up to the Captain to decide.

If he could make it up here in time, they could ride back down with pack horses to the North Platte and save a lot of travel by horseback. John worried a little about leaving the women and kids here with so few men to guard them. Pierre would be one more to stay, he didn't have any furs to trade at Rendezvous anyway.

The trappers were all getting excited about going to Rendezvous. They were looking forward to the fun. He had plenty of horses. The Indians were always stealing them from each other and trading them for whisky and powder and shot and stuff. He would have enough men riding with him for safety on the way down to the Green.

When the trappers started coming in with their winter catch, they would trade most of their pelts here for the better price. They would take some with them to trade for girls and whiskey. The girls there didn't understand money yet.

The supplies in the fort were holding up. Plenty of smoked meat, dried and smoked veggies and dried fruit for pies. With the good cooks he had here, life was good. Thank God for peace with the Indians. Even some small groups of Sioux had come to trade, saying that our prices were better than the other forts. Owning a steamboat saved a lot on freight. Maybe he should talk to the Captain about buying another one just in case one of his sank. With all of the dangers of river running, it might be a good idea. He would talk it over with Margaret.

Mark came in with an old Indian who had heard about his belief in people from other planets living here and claimed to be one of them. He told a story about a great round ship landing when he was a boy and some people getting off. John asked, "Did they stay?"

"Yes," the old man said, "They go live with Utes. The ship did not stay."

John didn't know whether to believe him or not. He told Mark to feed the old man and send him on his way. People might start to think that Brixton was a fort full of nuts.

Winter being almost over and the snow almost gone, things were picking up around the fort. With the lumber that Arco and Pierre were cutting at the mill, Mark was doing wonders making cabinets and furniture. They really did need more buildings, but the inside of the stockade was full. He had talked to Mark about adding on, but there was no time now. They had to get ready for Rendezvous. John was worried about leaving his family and the other wives while most of the men were gone. Talking it over with the trappers, he decided that the route he would take would be south and a little east and across the

Little Big Horn River. Then follow along the base of the mountains until he could go east until he hit the North Platte and follow it until he found the boat. The ice in the river had not broken up yet. Until it did the Shannon could not get to the North Platte.

Margaret came in, bent over, gave him a kiss on the head and sat down in the chair across from his desk. "Dove is pregnant again and Lisa thinks she might be too. And another thing: when the men clean out the stables have them haul it around to the garden area and spread it around. That soil is so rocky it needs all the help it can get."

"You may not get them to spread it. They are pretty independent, you know."

"You tell them if they don't do what I ask they won't get any pies or cookies next winter." John just laughed.

"In that case, I'm sure you will get what ever you want. You said the other two women were pregnant again but how about you?"

"No, not yet. Do you want to see your wife fat for nine months again?"

"Yes, I want a lot of kids, I was an only child and I was always jealous of others with siblings. You know that I am worried about leaving the fort with so few people to guard it while we are at Rendezvous. The trappers all want to go for the fun they have there. You can't blame them there but I worry about you and the other wives and the kids."

"I know and I am a little worried too, but things have been going quite well and I thought maybe you could get Lame Wolf to send a few people to help. I hear that they don't go to Rendezvous."

"That's a good idea, I'll ask Jack if he and Dove will ride up there and talk to him. I'm sure Dove would like to see her folks and tell them the news anyway."

The weather was beginning to warm up and some trappers were coming in with a small cache of furs to trade for things that they had run out of during the winter. One man had been run out of his camp by some Indians, and all he had time to grab was a small pack of furs and his rifle.

"Did the Indians get your whole winters catch?" John asked.

"No, I had all the rest cached. But they got all my camp gear. And my traps, and my pack horses."

"I'm sorry. I will give you the best price I can to replace what you lost." John took him over to the store and told Mark to give the man the things he needed at cost.

Mark had a book that John had made that gave the cost of everything in the store so he knew how much extra he had to get to make a profit. He thought John was a little too generous so he always made a little profit even when told to sell at cost. The trapper put his pack of furs on a work table. While Mark went through them the man picked out what he needed to replace his gear. After that was added up he still had a little money left so he filled a bag full of food. A sack of beans, a side of bacon, some jerky, coffee, flour, sugar, and a tin of lard.

"Do you have a pack horse I could have? I'll pay for him when I bring in my cache."

"Yes, we take in a lot of ponies. Go help yourself."

CHAPTER THIRTEEN
RENDEZVOUS

Spring came slowly to the little fort. Many came to trade their winter's catch of fur, beaver, mink, wolf, fox, wolverine, bison, and bear, both trappers and the different Indian tribes. There were even a few small groups of Sioux. There were so many trappers that Mark was worried that they might run out of whiskey. John had a still shipped in and set up but they didn't have enough grain to run it yet. They would grow more corn and wheat this year. It would probably be easier to have the grain shipped in than the whiskey.

Jack and Dove came to the office to say goodbye. Dove had little John all wrapped up and strapped in a pack for her to wear on her back. It wouldn't be right for a man to carry a baby. "We are taking some gifts for Lame Wolf that you are paying for. You know that he wouldn't like it if we didn't?"

"Yes, I want him to come stay for the time we are away."

When they had gone, John sat thinking about being gone from the fort for so long a time. Coonskin came in and slouched in a chair. He said, "As soon as we get the horses loaded we will be ready to go."

"I am still concerned about leaving the fort so deserted for so long a time."

"She is a beautiful woman and if I were in your shoes I wouldn't want to go off and leave her either. But after two or three Rendezvous you will be used to it and it won't bother you anymore. Besides, with the Blackfoot here no one will bother the fort."

"Yeah, I know you're right, but I still reserve the right to worry."

"What you need to worry about is how much old Lame Wolf is going to charge for his services."

In the morning, after the horses were loaded, John kissed his wife and baby goodbye, mounted up and rode out. The Blackfoot had not shown up so he was worried. He was the last to leave.

They didn't stop for lunch but rode through until dark. Two of the trappers, who had ridden on ahead had a fire going and a big pot of stew on to cook for supper. When John rode in the rest of the men were unloading the pack animals and picketing them out on the grass. John rode down to the river and let his horse drink. They had crossed the Bighorn River and would follow it to its headwaters then across south pass to the Rendezvous. John rode into camp and unsaddled and picketed his horse. He told Coonskin to set up a guard detail for the night; "If the Indians run off any horses we will play hell getting our merchandise to Rendezvous."

Frenchy noted that, "The river is going the wrong way or we could float the stuff there on a raft." Skinny responded, "That's great thinking; it's a wonder you don't have a Doctor's degree in something."

By daylight they were loaded up and moving south with some mountain on their left and the river on their right. When they reached South Pass John asked Coonskin, "How much farther?"

"Less than two days. If you push these horses any harder you'll wear a foot off their legs before we get there. I know you're having the young husband problems but no Indian tribe will attack your fort with a bunch of Blackfoot there. So quit worrying." At the fort, Lame Wolf and his wife and eight braves showed up two days after the trappers left. Everybody was happy to see them.

Little John was eight months old and walking so they had to keep an eye on him to keep him from going down to the river and feeding the fish. He couldn't swim. Lame Wolf only asked for half of the merchandise in the fort for his help. Dove told him what he could take and his squaw cut that down some.

Jim Bridger and his company of twelve men stopped by to trade for supplies on the way to Rendezvous. After he looked around the fort for a while Jim asked Mark, "How did you come to be friends with the Blackfoot; they don't cotton to white men much?"

"We brought a couple of their kids back to them who had been taken by trappers. The kids are the son and daughter of one of their head men and he was grateful. In fact that is them out there now."

"That's old Lame Wolf. I guess that's one of their head men. You picked the right guy to make friends with."

Mark asked Jim to take a message to John at Rendezvous that all is well at the fort.

Jim Bridger and his men got to Rendezvous six days after John and his men. Jim rode right to John's tent to give him Mark's message. He introduced himself; "You sure built you a fine post there. I like the way you set it all up. And having old Lame Wolf watch the place while you're gone, that is real smart. How did you get that to happen?"

"His daughter is married to one of our trappers and Grandpa likes to come see his grandson."

"So that pretty girl he was talking to is his daughter. I can see why some trapper wanted to marry her."

At Rendezvous there was always a big ruckus going on so it was noisy. Before Jim finished talking there was a shot fired and a lot of yelling. A trapper came over to report that, "Carson just shot the Swede and their boys are about to start shooting each other. Jim, you might be able to stop it but you better hurry." Jim yelled for some of his men to follow him and headed for the trouble. John told Skinny to watch the booth and ran after them.

They pushed their way through the crowd until they were between the two groups. Everybody knew Jim Bridger so when he raised his hand for silence they quieted down some. Jim asked "What's going on?"

Someone yelled that Carson shot the Swede and they were going to hang him.

"Why did Carson shoot the Swede?" The yelling started again.

Jim turned to Carson and asked, "Why did you shoot the Swede?"

"He came after me with his Green River knife; he was too big for me to fight so I shot him."

"Who saw this?" A lot of people started talking. John stepped forward and raised his hand for quiet. When he got a little quiet, he said,

"One person at a time. You." as he pointed at a big trapper he had seen at his fort. The man said," Kit was talking to the Swede's squaw and he didn't like it so he went after Kit with the knife."

Another said, "A fight is a fight but shooting the guy is no good."

Jim said, "Okay, let's take a vote. How many think Kit should hang? Raise your hands." About a quarter of the men raised their hand so Jim said, "Okay, stop shooting people, Kit. Let's go to John's booth and have a drink."

The trappers had a lot of respect for Jim. He wasn't a factor, one of the traders, but he had more than twenty men in his brigade and people listened when he talked so there was no more trouble.

Trading was brisk at John's booth so he didn't get to watch all the fun. There were horse races, shooting matches, squaw chasing, and all kinds of gambling games. Most of the trappers bought their supplies for the next season first, then did their gambling and squaw chasing.

At the end of the first week some of the sellers ran out of goods and started packing up to haul their furs to St. Louis. They wanted to get there early to get higher prices. John didn't have to as he would ship all the way to England. At the end of the second week John packed up. Two of the men that had come with them were ready to go. They had spent all their money and were glad to get paid to help to get the furs to the river. Skinny Wilson asked if he could bring a squaw with them. He had traded his ponies for her and only had one left to ride but that was okay because the squaw could walk. John said that was okay because they had so many furs to haul to the river that they would all have to load their own horses and walk with the squaw.

The woman was Nez Perce from up north and had a name that Skinny couldn't pronounce so he called her Darlene. She had a large pack of her belongings. When they moved out they all had large packs to carry. They only had a two day walk to the Sweetwater River where he hoped the Shannon would be waiting for them. Mr. and Mrs. Wilson led the way up over the South pass and down to the river. The boat couldn't get as far up the river as John had hoped and it took three days of walking to get there. They were all happy to see her sitting there with smoke curling from her stack. Her crew was loading fire wood when they came up. The Captain watched from the second deck rail as the people walking and the long line of pack horses coming along the shore.

John gave orders to unpack the horses and start hauling the packs aboard. Then he joined the Captain above; they went into the Captain's cabin to talk. Before they got started though the Captain told John, "You had better have those packs put in the cabins and boat storage or there won't be room for the horses on the lower deck." John went out on the cat walk and gave that order then ordered them to save a cabin for the Wilsons and one for him, too. The men could sleep in the salon.

When all was loaded the men had to cut a lot of hay for the horses for the trip home. They could have unloaded them at night to forage, but there was danger of Indians walking off with them.

It was a long trip by river to get home, about twelve hundred miles by river and less than three hundred by land, so John and the Captain decided that it wasn't worth it. They came up with a plan.

CHAPTER FOURTEEN
THE HOMECOMING

It was a long ride home so John and Captain Small had plenty of time to plan. Captain Small said, "There is a small steam boat for sale at Fort Kiowa just south of the big bend. The owner was killed by our old friends, the Rees. We could load all the fur packs on it and send it to Ohio now. The Shannon is overloaded and overworked. We could use another boat. Do you have enough money with you to buy it?"

John laughed. "Probably not. A lot of the trappers wanted money for their furs. How much did they want for it?"

"Two thousand. If you don't have enough, the boat does. We have been doing well hauling freight and people back and forth so we have it."

What about a crew for it?"

"The owner was the Captain so you could promote the Pilot and hire a new one in St. Louis."

"The next thing I know you will be telling me that we need a shipping office in St. Louis."

"No, but it would be good to have an agent in Wheeling."

"Yes, I have been thinking the same thing. Then I start to think maybe some wagons and teamsters and guards then I think how about a ship to come up the Mississippi and ship from St. Louis straight to England? Then I wonder if I'm not going crazy." They both laughed and decided to have a drink. The Captain thought that those were all good ideas.

When they got to Ft. Kiowa it was almost dark. As they came up the river John could see the small steamer tied to the bank below the fort. As they came along side John had the Captain pull over close enough to jump across to the deck of the Frog. We may have to rename this one, he thought.

There was a guard with a rifle on the shore side of the deck but as John walked toward him he saw people in the salon and turned and went in. The guard walked in behind John. The three men stood and John introduced himself. "I am John Brix. I own the Shannon. Captain Small said this boat is for sale. Who do I talk to about it?" A tall thin man stepped forward with his hand out and took John's hand and pumped it hard, "I am Ned Jones, Pilot." He introduced the rest of the men and they all sat down. Mr. Jones said, "The Frog was owned by the Captain and he was killed by Indians while hunting for some fresh meat. He has a wife but going through the ship's papers we found a will. It says if anything happened to him to sell the boat and send the money to his wife. So we put the boat up for sale." They talked for a while about the Captain, the boat, the work the boat was doing and her condition. Then there was a yell from shore and they all went out on deck. It was Captain Small, Jim Brown the pilot, and John Paterson the engineer. The gang plank was run out and they came aboard. Ned Jones and Jim Brown were old friends. Mr. Jones took everyone on a tour of the Frog. When they all got back to the salon Captain Small gave Ned the money to buy the boat and while they were doing the paperwork to transfer the title Captain Small announced, "With my approval, Mr. Brix has decided to make you Captain of the Frog and ask you to hire a Pilot when you get to St. Louis, if that is all right with you." Ned was very happy with that. John told him to pull the Frog up beside The Shannon to transfer the fur packs and get ready to head down river.

They all stayed on board while the boat was moved and tied to the Shannon then everyone got busy moving fur packs and enough supplies to run the boat to Wheeling. John wrote letters to Mr. Parks in Boston and Mr. Samson, the freighter, telling them about the new boat and instructions on using it.

John called Skinny Wilson in. "I need a man to go with the Frog as hunter and guard. How about showing Darlene St. Louis and the big city of Wheeling? I have told the Captain to give you money to spend on the way. What do you say?"

"Yes sir, Darlene has liked riding the boat but I am sure she will like the long trip."

With the first grey light of dawn, the two boats headed out in opposite directions. The Frog down stream, and the Shannon north for the

Yellowstone. The Shannon stopped for the night and at all the forts on the way: Fort Pierre, Tilton, Berthold, and Union. John was getting a little anxious about getting home. He was worried about his family and whether his fort was still standing, and at the very least whether he had anything left to sell after old Lame Wolf went home. So as they came in sight of the fort he had the men fire one of the swivel guns to alert them.

When they were tied up to the pier the whole fort was there to meet them. As soon as the plank was in place John ran down it and into his wife's arms. She said, "I thought you were dead. Trappers coming through from Rendezvous said it was over weeks ago. I was checking out replacements."

"How did that go for you?"

"Not too well. None of them could read."

Two wagons were brought to the pier while the horses were being unloaded. While the supplies were being offloaded, John and Margaret and Captain Small went to the office where Mark Smith waited for them and they went over the books for the Rendezvous. Things were good.

CHAPTER FIFTEEN
GOOD TIMES

Things were real good. The gardens around the fort were growing well. The boat had brought in grain to make whiskey and to plant. John had ordered farm equipment such as plows and harrows, and Arco was breaking more ground to plant. By the end of summer they had added onto the fort and were building a structure for a church and a school. Now that all of the women were pregnant they were going to need a school. When the Frog came in they found out that Skinny's wife Darlene was pregnant, too.

Another man and his wife came with the Frog too so the population was growing. This fellow's name was Paul Lyton. He was a blacksmith who had all his tools and some supplies for his trade. When Captain Jones and John came down from the Captain's cabin, the Captain introduced John to the Lytons. "You will be happy to know, John, that he is a smith with tools and some supplies."

"That does make me happy. We have a shop set up for you, but a house won't be finished for a few more days. You will have to stay on the boat or stay in the bunkhouse with a bunch of single men. How's that for a choice?"

Mrs. Lyton laughed. "The boat will be just fine for me."

John asked, "Did you bring any furniture?"

Mr. Lyton said, "Not much, a bed, two dressers, two kitchen chairs and two trunks of clothing. We would have brought more but the Captain here wanted too much for freight."

Jack Valines and Skinny Wilson brought the wagons down and backed them onto the dock to unload the Frog of all the supplies. Mark came with his check list. Margaret and Lisa came to the dock to meet the new people. John introduced them to the Lytons and to Skinny's wife Darlene. He commented, "Mrs. Lyton, all the women here at the fort are with child. It seems to be something catching so be careful."

Darlene added, "Me, too." Mrs. Lyton said, "I'm not. How many women and children are here? We thought I would be the only white woman here." Margaret answered, "Well, you two make six women. We have five children. Two girls and three boys and five pregnant women. So before long, if everything comes out okay, we will have ten children at our little fort."

Margaret took the Lytons and Darlene on a tour of the fort while John and Captain Jones went to the office to go over the books. After going over the profit and lost figures on the trip, the Captain handed John a sack of money saying, "I don't feel good about having all this extra money on the boat with me and it's your money so you should have it."

"Do you have enough to take care of your needs on the boat?"

"Yes, plenty, and the other forts pay me in cash for hauling their freight so I always have some coming in."

John dumped the bag on the desk and counted it. He handed back ten double eagles; "Keep that in case you need it. I want you to buy a swivel gun and two or three mounts when you get to St. Louis. They work real well to discourage the Indians from attacking you."

That evening at supper, after John said grace, he introduced the Lytons. "Paul is a blacksmith and will be a welcome addition to our town. We will need some help finishing a house for them while he gets the shop set up." After dinner Captain Jones went to the office with John and informed him that he would like to head down river as soon as possible before the river dropped too much.

John immediately got everyone who was any good as a carpenter to work on the house, and the rest to get the boat loaded with the fur, the hides, and the smoked meat to sell down river. He had letters to send with the Frog so he went on board to see the Captain. He found him in the salon going over some books. He handed him the mail.

"I'm thinking of finding an agent in St. Louis not so much for selling but for handling freight shipped direct from England to be sent here by the boats so if you think of someone you could talk to them while you're there. I have written to the shipper to see if he will go to St. Louis and what the costs would be."

"Yes, I can see that it would save all that wagon hauling from Baltimore. It will save money. You could ask the trappers; they all know the people to trust in St. Louis. Most of them probably owe them money."

Later, John was going over the books in his office when Margaret came in. After seating herself, she said, "John, the women here have some things that we need. Do you have time for me to tell you now?" He looked up from his book, leaned back in his chair, smiled at his beautiful wife and answered, "If the list is long I probably won't remember. It would be better if you make a list. Get the girls all together and make a big list of everything you can think of. We certainly want to keep our women happy."

"But John, if you buy everything we can think of it will cost a lot. I know a wife is not to know her husbands business, but I can't help worrying. How are we doing financially?" John smiled.

"You are right. Women are not told their husband's business because they talk too much but we are doing fine. The boats are making money and some extra by hauling for the other forts along the river. We have done well on the fur trade. So you can buy anything you want. I've been thinking about going to St. Louis or even to New Orleans to contract with an agent to handle our shipments from England instead of shipping overland from Baltimore. I have written to Captain Wright and the shipping company about coming up the

Mississippi. Do you think a pregnant lady could stand a long boat ride and a busy trip?"

"Oh, John. That would be wonderful. I'm just sorry that the Smiths can't go too; that would be so much fun

"Yes, but I can't do without them. Mark handles all of the business of the fort. And Lisa runs the chow hall. I just can't do without them. Jack is learning to be Marks assistant, and Dawn and Darlene are doing most of the cooking. In another year, if you girls could keep from getting pregnant, we could all go together."

Margaret laughed. "Maybe if you and Mark learned the facts of life we might be able to do that."

When the Shannon came up the river the wagons were waiting on the docks and everybody from the fort was waiting to unload it. Captain Small came to the rail. "I'm glad you are in a hurry. We had trouble with low water coming up this time." John went aboard; they went to the Captain's cabin where John announced, "Margaret and I and Charley are going with you down the river this time. I want to find an agent in St. Louis or in New Orleans to handle freight coming from England direct. I have written to the shipping company to see what the cost would be. It might be cheaper than hauling from Baltimore."

The Captain said, "Now that Lafitte has moved on to Texas, it is a lot safer. It should be cheaper. I am not going to make it back up here this year the way the river is dropping."

"We will come back on the Frog. It draws a lot less water. Charley will like the boat ride and Margaret has a long list of things the women want from the city."

Just then Margaret stuck her head in the door and asked," Can I come in or is this for men only?" Both men got to their feet; the Captain said, "Come in, Mrs. Brix. Pretty women are always welcome in my bed chamber."

"I don't know whether to be embarrassed or flattered." They all sat down and talked of the coming trip. When she got up to leave, the Captain asked, "Do you plan to make it back to the fort in time to have that baby? Or will you have it on the Frog?"

"I hope we make it back in time; if not John will have to deliver it."

John quickly assured him, "We'll hurry." He studied his wife with a worried look on his face, "Maybe we should take another woman with us."

She just laughed, "We'll hurry."

John decided right then that Jack and Dove would go along. He didn't even want to think about delivering a baby.

Soon the Shannon was loaded with furs, hides, and smoked meat to trade along the way. John went over everything with Mark. "You know we have done real well here. I think it would be a good idea to give each man and yourself a bonus, the amount depending on the amount of work they do. Make sure you give yourself the most. I've been thinking about making you a partner in the fort; that way you will get a percentage of all the fort's profits which is only fair since you run it." He gave Mark the paperwork to sign making him a twenty five percent partner. The next day the total population of the fort was on the dock to say goodbye to the family. As the boat left the dock the two swivel guns were fired as a salute.

They stopped at all the forts on the way down the river to take on freight and passengers which gave John, Margaret and Charley a chance to see how they all were doing and to meet the people they didn't know. Dove and Jack had come along. Dove was cooking and Jack and John were hunting. The two little boys, John and Charley, were under Margaret's care; they stayed mostly in the salon.

At Fort Union John and Margaret went to see the post commander, a Colonel Jack Duvall. They were escorted into his office by a private in a dirty uniform. They introduced themselves. The Colonel said, "So you have the new post down on the Yellowstone. I have heard you are doing well and have even been trading with the Blackfoot. That's impressive."

"Thank you. A Blackfoot girl is married to one of our men, and is cooking for us on this trip. The only fighting we've done is with the Sioux and after that little fracas some have come to trade. We feel real lucky and are happy about it."

Margaret added, "We bought two Blackfoot children from some trappers in St. Louis and returned them home to their families so the Blackfoot have forgiven us for being white."

The Colonel laughed. "That has got to be a first. I didn't think they liked anyone. How about having lunch with us? It's just army chow but it won't make you sick.

"That's kind of you sir but how about joining us on the boat? Our cook is very good, and there are fresh vegetables and great pie for dessert."

So they went down to the boat with Margaret holding up her skirts to keep them from dragging in the dust of the parade ground. On arriving at the Shannon they went to the salon for lunch and walked into some trouble. Jack Valines and one of the boat crew were holding a big trapper and Captain Small was facing them holding a pistol.

The trapper demanded, "What the hell? I just wanted to rent that squaw for a while. What's wrong with that?"

"She is Jack's wife and if you plan to ride down the river on this boat you better mind your manners or you will end up feeding the fish along with the dead buffalo." The grumbling trapper sat down at a table to wait for lunch. John, Margaret, and the Colonel sat at a table near him. He looked over at them, "Hey, a white woman." John produced a pistol from his belt and said, "Get off the boat."

"Who do you think you are, ordering me around? I paid for a ride down to St. Louis and I ain't going to be throwed off."

The Captain gathered some of his men, walked over to the trapper and standing very close to him and said, "That man owns this boat and if he says for you to get off the boat, I will give you the choice to walk off on your own, or be thrown off. Then I will give you your money back." The big trapper got slowly to his feet, picked up his pack and rifle and left the boat. The Colonel said, "That man is always trouble. If you had shot him we all would be better off."

The meal was good, a smoked buffalo roast, some fresh caught fish, and apple cobbler and cider. The Colonel said it was the best he had eaten in a long while, that he would eat on the boat whenever it was at the fort.

They were soon on their way. The river was running a little low so twice they had to grasshopper over sand bars but they made it past the Ree village without any trouble. They passed the Cannonball River and were almost to the Cheyenne River when during lunch the boat lurched; there was a tearing sound from below. The Pilot, while yelling something from the wheelhouse, swung the boat toward the west bank to run it up onto a large sandbar. Even though they were prepared for it the sudden stop it almost knocked everybody down. Captain Small ran up to the wheelhouse to find out what was up. Jim Brown, the Pilot, met him and informed him that, "A hidden log tore a hole on the port side about a foot from the keel." Mr. Patterson, the engineer, added, "We were taking on water pretty fast so we opened the steam valves to try to stop the cold water from blowing the boiler but it's a good idea to abandon ship, just in case."

Captain Small came back down to the salon to announce, "The crew is getting the gangplank out and there is some danger of the boiler blowing, so everyone should get as far away from the boat as fast as you can until the danger is past."

John grabbed Charley and his wife and headed for shore. He grabbed a rifle on the way out as did Jack and Dove. Jack had little John by the hand. Once everyone was off and far enough away to be safe, John told Jack to watch for Indians and went to talk to Mr. Patterson. "Well, it looks like you saved the boat. How long before it will be safe to go back on board?"

"We had better wait an hour just to be safe. We have lumber on board to patch the hole but we will have to careen her to get at it so we will have to plan to sleep ashore."

Two hours later the crew had camp set up in a grove of trees and all the men were unloading the boat. Everything moveable was hauled ashore to lighten the boat for careening. The women set up a kitchen and started preparing some food. Block and tackle set ups were brought out and hooked up to roll the boat up on her side to repair the bottom. It took the rest of the afternoon with even the women pulling on the ropes to get it up far enough to do the job.

Guards were posted to watch for trouble but they also had to keep track of two little boys so they wouldn't run off. That night Margaret was sitting on a log by the fire with Charley asleep on her lap; she was thinking about all that had happened to them since she and John had met in London. She wondered if she hadn't met John where would she be now. Probably still selling flowers and being poor as a church mouse. Here they were with bags of money, shipwrecked in Indian country and liable to be scalped any minute. Jack came in from guard duty and sat down near her. She asked him if he had seen anything.

"No, I walked out a mile or so but no fresh tracks."

It took two days to replace the damaged planks, caulk and paint with hot pitch then they let it roll back upright and pumped the water out. That took more time. They had to grasshopper it off the sandbar and reload it. They had lost a few days but were on their way again.

The log shows that the Shannon met the Frog at Fort Kiowa just below the big bend. They had dinner together aboard the Shannon and in the morning both boats were on their way. Three weeks later they were in sight of St. Louis. That night John asked the whole crew to have dinner with him and his wife before going ashore. With everyone there he asked them to be quiet and he led them in prayer. "We thank you, Lord, for helping us make this trip down the river. We all know the danger we were in when the boat was disabled. There is a long list of things that could have happened and we are sure, at least I am sure, that you kept us safe. Thank you for the food. In Jesus' name we pray. Amen

CHAPTER SIXTEEN
ST. LOUIS

Once the Shannon was tied to a dock, John headed into town to arrange for a warehouse and wagons to haul and store the furs and hides. He went up town to the post office to see if there was mail for him. After collecting the mail, mostly from the shipping company, he saw a bulletin board and found among the notices some for warehouse space. One was on the water with a pier. One of the notices had wagons and teams for sale so he decided to go there first. He asked a passerby for directions and headed off. St. Louis at the time was a melting pot of people so the fact that he was dressed in buckskins with two pistols and a long skinning knife in his belt didn't cause any strange looks. On finding the wagon yard he at first saw no one around. Then a man came out of a barn and started greasing an axle on a light wagon. When John walked over the man looked up; "Is there something I can do for you?"

"Yes, I am in need of a wagon and team."

"To buy or rent?"

"To rent now and buy tomorrow."

"Well, look around and see if there is something here that you like. There are more out back."

John found a buckboard with a back seat bolted on and thought that would be good for hauling people around town while they did their business. So he bought the wagon and the best team of horses the man had and headed back to the boat.

He backed the wagon down onto the dock just to see how the team worked. The women and the two little boys climbed up into the back seat while the Captain and Jack got in beside John. They headed off to find the warehouse that they needed. As they drove through town Margaret was watching how everybody dressed; "John, you should have changed out of your buckskins before driving through town."

"It's fine. People will just think I'm your servant; that's what I feel like most of the time anyway."

"Just for that I'm going to buy three new outfits while we are here."

They found the building. It had a for sale or rent sign on the front. It was two stories with a pier in the river behind it. They weren't there long before a man showed up; he introduced himself as Carl James, the agent for the selling of the building. John introduced everyone to Mr. James who opened the building as they all trooped in. The first floor was all warehouse space but the second floor was set up as a manufacturing space with some living quarters. The women went to go through the living quarters while John, the Captain and Mr. James went into the second floor office to discuss the price of the place. The office furniture was still there although it was so old that it was probably not worth the hassle of selling it. When they were seated, John asked what they were asking for the place.

"The man who owned the place died and his wife wants to get rid of it so the price she is asking is quite reasonable. But I think any reasonable offer would be accepted. She's asking three thousand." John asked the Captain, "What do you think?"

"I think it is a good price. You will need someone to run it though."

"Have you someone in mind?" John knew that the Captain had been around here most of his life and knew a lot of people.

"I know a man who would be a good watchman. He lost a leg in the war but he gets around on a peg leg and he's a good fighting man. Name is Duncan."

"You mean Tom Duncan?" Mr. James asked.

"Yes, he's a good man. "He's an old pirate, at least he looks like one."

"Well, if you want this place the papers for the sale are at my house. I only live a few blocks away so I will go get them and be right back."

"If you like, ask Jack to drive you. He stayed with the wagon. Well, Captain, let's go see what my wife thinks of the place." They met

Margaret and Dove coming out of the living quarters.

"Well, dear, what do you think?"

"It's nicer than our place at the fort but I can't imagine hauling water up here all the time. Come look, I think you will be impressed."

When Mr. James came back they all went into the office to sign the papers for the sale. John undid his shirt and took out a money belt and they counted out three thousand dollars in gold coins.

His wife asked, "Do you have enough left to buy Dove and me and the boys some new clothes? If not you're in trouble."

Mr. James gave John the keys to the place and the deed and put the money in a satchel that he had brought back with him; after shaking hands all around, he left. They all followed him out and loaded onto the wagon. John locked up and climbed up beside his wife and they headed toward the small church; he jumped off, told Jack to pick him up there in an hour and went in. As John walked shopping district with Jack driving. As they drove through town John saw a down the aisle to the front of the seats a door beside the platform opened and a tall man in a black suit stepped out. He and John walked toward each other; they shook hands.

"I am the Rev. Carl Johnson, welcome to the Zion Baptist Church."

"I am John Brix of Brix and Co. We just bought a place of business here in town and have need of some people to work for us. I thought you might be able to recommend someone." The preacher thought for a minute, then said, "Yes I know a few people that you could talk to."

"Good, I also would like to know if you would marry a couple who work for me. She is an Indian"

"Yes, they are God's people, too." The preacher led John back into his office. When they were seated he asked, "What business are you in and what kind of jobs do you need people for?"

"We have a trading post up the river and two river steamers and a store in Boston so I need clerks and a manager and a warehousemen, and a night watchman. Although the Captain has recommended a man named Tom Duncan as the watchman; do you know him?"

Rev. Johnson laughed. "Most people think he's an old pirate, but I think he's honest.

"There is a young couple that will be here in church Sunday. They are camped somewhere out along the river. They both clerked in a big store in Baltimore. There are two clerks in one package for you. I don't know how to get in touch with them but if you come to church on Sunday I could introduce you."

"That is a sneaky way to get people to come to church, but we'll be here. How soon can you marry my friends?"

"How about Saturday morning?"

"What time?"

"Ten."

"We'll be here."

John left the church feeling good about the talk with the preacher. He knew Jack wanted a church wedding for Dove and himself. And Margaret would love getting ready for it. He would catch hell for not giving her more time to get ready but it would save him money.

Rev. Johnson came out of the church and they stood talking about the town until the wagon came back. John introduced the preacher to everybody and then told Jack that the pastor would marry him and Dove Saturday morning here at the church if that was okay. Jack looked at Dove and they both nodded. But Margaret turned to John and said, "You dirty rat, you know that only gives us two days to get ready. You just think it will save you money by not giving us much time. You just watch me. You'll be sorry." John started to climb onto the wagon but she pushed him off and grabbed the whip and whipped the horses. She yelled, "You can walk back to the boat." The horses took off but John jumped on the back of the wagon as it passed. He waved to the surprised preacher. Jack grabbed the whip from Margaret and fought the horses down to a trot. Everyone was laughing except Margaret. The Captain was riding in the back seat with Dove and the boys. John reached up and tapped him on the back while quietly instructing him to jump off, which they both did the next time they slowed for cross street traffic. As they stepped up on the sidewalk he explained why they had left the wagon. "The preacher said that Duncan is a good man. Do you think you can find him?"

"Yeah, he hangs out at a bar down by the river. If he isn't there we can leave a message for him. While we're there, how about moving the Shannon to our dock? It will save some dock fees."

"Good idea. We could start unloading." They walked on down to the river area and found the bar where Duncan hung out. It was only a few blocks from their warehouse. They went in but it was a dark and gloomy place. Before they could see anything a voice boomed out, "Hello Captain, you are just in time to buy me a drink." A big peg legged man stumped over out of the gloom. Captain Small shook hands with him, introduced him to John, "We might have a job for you if you're interested."

"Aye, I do need some work. I ain't had any in a while. No one wants a one legged man."

"Come along then to the boat and you can see what you think of the job." So off they went to the boat. On arrival, John found a man who was hanging around the dock and gave him a dollar to tell Jack that they had moved the boat to their own dock. He then jumped aboard before the gangplank was pulled in. As the boat moved away from the dock John went to the salon to talk to Duncan. As he walked in he heard the Captain telling Duncan, "We need a night watchman for a warehouse we bought. It has living quarters so you don't have to live elsewhere. We are coming up to the place now. I'll see you later. John can tell you the rest, I am needed in the wheelhouse."

Once they were tied off and the warehouse was unlocked John took Duncan on a grand tour. While they were going through the small apartment John said, "I think there will be a young couple living in the other apartment. You can probably get them to feed you if you offer to buy some food now and then."

Tom asked, "How much is the pay going to be? If I could get a little advance on my pay I have some bills to pay, having not worked for a while." John gave him sixty dollars and told him to get a shotgun and ammo from the boat. Duncan took off then to get his things and pay his bills. John went back to the boat for lunch. On the way Captain Small met him and advised him, "If you are going for lunch, the cooks are off shopping. There is a good little restaurant just a block from here, I'll even buy."

"That is something new. I didn't even know you ever carried money."

"Oh, I don't mind spending money, It is yours anyway."

Saturday came with a lot of bustle; Dove, looking very beautiful in a very pretty dress, married Jack and became Mrs. Valines. It was all paid for by John. The next day the whole crew went to church except Duncan and one seaman to watch the Shannon. After the service Pastor Johnson introduced John to George and Sylvia Grey, the young couple who would like jobs as clerks.

John was pleased with his first impressions of the couple and asked them to follow them to the warehouse to see the operation and to have lunch on the boat. They had driven their wagon into town for church for fear of someone taking all of their belongings while they were gone.

While John showed the Greys the warehouse and explained the operation to them Dove and Margaret went on board the Shannon to prepare lunch.

On completion of the grand tour John asked the Greys if they had any questions. Mr. Grey answered, "Yes, will there be funds available for work on the building? And how much is our pay to be?"

"Forty dollars a month for you and thirty for your wife plus a percentage on the sales of merchandise, but that won't be until the ship comes in from England or overland from Baltimore. And yes there will be funds for maintenance on the building. I want a stable built on the south side of the building big enough for five horses and high enough for hay storage above. And I want Brix Co. in big letters painted on both ends of the building with *merchandise* in smaller letters on the street end. As soon as the Frog comes in you will have merchandise to sell so you need to get shelves and the stable built and the signs painted right away. Check with the preacher to recommend people to do the work. I expect you to manage the operation here and your wife to help with the books and be a clerk. But you will hire help as needed. You can start right after lunch." He smiled all the time he talked. At lunch Mrs. Grey said to Margaret, "This sounds like a big operation. I hope we will be able to do it to your husband's satisfaction."

"Don't worry. John has all the books set up for you. Mostly it is for shipping freight up the river and the furs to England. The store is just to defray the cost some. If you have any trouble tell the steamboat captains; if they don't know what to do they will get a message to John."

With lunch done, they sat around talking in the salon, getting better acquainted. Just relaxing on a Sunday afternoon.

After breakfast Monday, Jack hitched the team to the wagon and took the back seat off for hauling lumber. John and George Grey went around to some lumber yards. He loaded lumber for shelves and ordered lumber for the stable. When they returned to the warehouse Jack helped them unload the lumber so that they could go get a load of hay for the horses.

Margaret and Mrs. Grey worked in the office going over the way John did the books and getting the office set up for business. By the end of the week, the shelves were done and the men were working on the stables and the signs were painted. The next week the Shannon left for New Orleans and the Frog came in with supplies from Baltimore. The shelves were stocked with the goods that John thought would sell here in St. Louis. John was satisfied that everything was done that he needed to do and prepared to board the Frog to go home. He gathered everyone in the office of the warehouse and made a going away speech. He said, "I'm sure that the Lord has sent us the best people he had available to run this end of the business. We are happy to have met all of you and will remember you in our prayers. If you need anything ask the boat captains. We may not be back this way again so may God bless you and keep you and let his light shine upon you and give you good business. Amen."

"Shame on you, John," Margaret said. "I want to add that I have enjoyed being here with you and will keep you all in my heart as we head up the Missouri to home. Goodbye."

They boarded the boat. It headed out.

CHAPTER SEVENTEEN
GOING BACK HOME

As the Frog headed up the river, the Greys and Tom Duncan stood on the pier and watched. George said, "Well, we have a big job to do. I think we should put up notices around town that we are open for business. I think we should hire a warehouseman and a teamster to move all this merchandise.

Mr. Duncan, do you need anything for your apartment?"

"Well, maybe some furniture. A bed would be nice and a table and chairs."

"I'll give you some money to get what you need. Take the wagon and stop and tell the Preacher that we need a couple of men, and then you should get some sleep; you have the night shift." As George handed him the money he said, "Bring me receipts. Mr. Brix wants everything accounted for. He said that whatever you needed would be paid for by the company." Duncan just nodded and stumped out.

Captain Jones and John and Margaret were sitting in the Captain's cabin having a glass of wine and talking about all that had happened in St. Louis. The Captain said, "I think you got a good start there. I liked those people you hired. Have you got word whether or not the sailing ship will come up the Mississippi?"

"Yes, the answer came in on the Shannon from Wheeling; they will give it a try. A ship is on its way so as soon as we get home you need to unload and load up and get back with what furs and hides we have. Do you think you can make another run before winter?"

"I'm not sure; if we get some rain and we don't get an early freeze up we'll be okay."

Margaret said, "It seems to me that with all the supplies we have on board that we should not have any needs this winter at the fort. The warehouse in St. Louis is loaded with fur to be shipped to England. I can't see any reason to worry unless you spent too much money in St. Louis and are running short." They all laughed.

"It was you and Dove buying all those clothes that spent all our money. You are right, though; we really don't need anything, but I hate to think of all of that good merchandise coming in on the ship just sitting in the warehouse all winter."

"Maybe they will sell it all this winter. I think the Greys will try to make it pay. They seem like good people."

They had picked up a few trappers heading back to the mountains and an Army officer and his wife with three troopers for Fort Union at the mouth of the Yellowstone. They had also picked up a lot of mail and some freight for all of the forts. One of the deck hands came and knocked at the door. When the Captain opened the door, the deck hand said there was about to be a fight between the troopers and the trappers. John went down to the salon. He met the officer, a Lt. Carson, on the way. They opened the door to the salon and walked into the middle of it. A trapper and a trooper were circling around with knives. John pulled a pistol from his belt, walked right between them and told the trooper to put up the knife and back down or be thrown overboard. The trapper said, "Who are you to threaten to throw us overboard?" A deckhand who was watching the fight spoke up with, "He owns this boat and if he says so you would be swimming to Fort Union."

John warned the trapper, "We have a long trip ahead of us so keep the peace or I will leave you at the first stop we make."

Lt. Carson added, "The Army would not like that."

"The Army just pays enough to cover the food your boys eat. It wouldn't be a loss if you went by some other boat, if you could find one that would take you. If you trappers start any more trouble you will be walking to the Yellowstone."

Lt. Carson ordered, "There will be no more trouble from the Army. We don't want to walk or eat our own cooking. Your boat's cooking is I think the best I've ever tasted and I will hang anyone who messes that up for me."

Captain Jones had some freight for Fort Randall so while there they loaded some fire wood, two more trappers came on board for a ride on credit. They had sold furs to John before and they had no horses. They had sold them for money to last the winter. There were no empty cabins so they had to sleep on the deck which was no great discomfort to trappers. John was a little worried about the late season and how low the river was going to be running. It would mean a slow trip up the river and his wife with a baby coming. They stayed the night tied up there. When they woke up in the morning, the river had risen some during the night. Captain Jones said at breakfast that it must have rained some up stream. Margaret asked, "Do you think it will keep rising, at least enough to get us home without walking?"

"We haven't had a full weather report from that old Indian up on the Yellowstone yet, so we don't know for sure. As soon as we get his report I'll let you know, Mrs. Brix." The river did rise for a couple of days. That made John and Captain Jones very happy as it made for a safer and faster run home.

It was almost dark that day when a deckhand yelled up at the wheel house that there is a big canoe up ahead. "It looks empty. Maybe it got away from someone." As it drew closer they could see that it had two men laying down and hidden by the sides. One was an Indian and the other a trapper.

When they drew closer the Pilot slowed the boat and pulled over close. The two men leaned out and grabbed the sides; they tied on. One of the trappers jumped in and checked the bodies. The trapper was dead. The Indian was still alive, but badly wounded. They got a couple of buffalo robes and some bandages, made a bed there on the deck for the Indian and started working on him. He had a bullet hole through him just below the left collar bone but he had lost a lot of blood. John came to see what was going on. One of the trappers said that the Indian was a Sioux and it might be better to just throw him in the river.

"No, we are not on real good terms with the Sioux. Maybe this will help if he makes it. He doesn't look too good, though. When we tie up tonight we will take the trapper ashore and bury him. Does anybody know who he is?"

"No."

It must have been a big storm up the river that kept the water high enough to make a good run. They stopped at all the posts on the way up and did a lot of trading with them because they all knew it would be the last boat up the river this year. Every post wanted kegs of whisky. John almost sold out; he hoped that they had got that still running while he was gone. Those trappers could get pretty mean when they ran out.

At Fort Union they said goodbye to Lt. Carson and his troopers and left some supplies for the fort. Colonel Duvall came down to have lunch and say hello, "The food is so good on your boats that I am going to eat on them every time one stops here. I suppose I will have to go hungry until spring."

"The Frog will be going out in a few days. I'm sure they will stop here on the way out. So you can get one more meal before winter." John told the Colonel about the Sioux Indian they had picked up; after lunch he took him to see him. The Colonel spoke Sioux so he asked him what had happened. The Indian spoke slowly and long. When he was done, Colonel Duvall and John went back to the salon so he could tell everyone the story. "His name is Walking Buffalo. The trapper was Whisky Jack; he didn't know his last name. He said that Jack lived with the Sioux and had a squaw. They decided to go to a Crow village and steal some horses. Someone spotted them and they had to run for it. They got to their canoe and shoved off but the Crow were too close behind them. He turned to fire at them and got shot. Jack was still paddling. Then Jack was hit. That's the last he remembers until he woke up on this boat. He doesn't know why he is still alive. He was sure someone would have thrown him in the river and kept their guns."

John told everyone, "When he is up to it we will give him his gun and a horse and he can go home. We had a fight with them but some small groups are trading with us now. They lost the fight but don't seem to hold a grudge."

"Oh they won't forget that fight. I heard about it. It is what they call a remembered fight.

They say they lost a lot of men, that you used cannon and that they didn't know that you even had cannon."

"We don't; they were swivel guns but the effect is devastating to mounted warriors. We only lost one man in that little scrap. I think they lost about twenty and a lot of wounded. We'll send old Walking Buffalo home in good shape and will even throw in a chunk of smoked elk to take to his family."

"You need to quit being so generous. It makes our trader look bad." "We are a long way up the river, we can't hurt your business much."

In the first light of the next day they left for home. It was a week before they reached home. They had to stop at the other posts along the way to deliver mail and to trade. When they came in sight of the fort they fired a swivel gun to alert everyone that they were back. Everyone was out there waiting when they tied up to the dock. After all the hugging and hand shaking John and Margaret went up together with Charley to their house. It was nice to be home. Everybody else spent the rest of the day unloading the boat. With two wagons it only took three trips to the store rooms to get it all.

Walking Buffalo was well enough to walk to the fort. Skinny Wilson spoke; he showed him to a bunk in the bunkhouse. Skinny then took him to the pony herd and told him to pick out a pony for himself. Walking Buffalo looked a long time at Skinny then asked, "Is this what big chief say?"

"Yes, and some smoked elk to take to squaw." Then Walking Buffalo turned, walked to the herd, picked out a horse and led it back to Skinny. They went back to the fort. Skinny led the horse to the barn, put it in a stall and forked some hay into the manger. Then Skinny took Walking Buffalo to the mess hall for dinner.

After dinner John told all the men and any women that were interested to come to his office; he had something to show them. When they arrived, he had a big map of the area hung on the wall. It was a map of the Yellowstone River that came all the way from Washington. As people came in they went over and looked at it. John said, "We have put in to the government to get title to some land here. I have put in for a half section here where the fort is. I have paid for the land but you can homestead some if you want. You can get a hundred and sixty acres that way for free. There are rules you have to go by to do that but I have all the forms here and will help you go through it. You need to decide which piece you want and we'll draw it out on the map so that we don't ask for the same piece."

Arco asked, "Can a Negro get land too?"

"I checked into that and they said if he is free then yes. Do you have a place in mind, Mr. Elk?"

"I will wait and pick someplace nobody else did pick, sir."

"That's a good idea. One of these ornery old trappers might shoot you for your land. I think everyone who is going to get some land should do it now before the boat sails so that the paperwork can go with it and be recorded during the winter. The boat will leave in three days so get it done."

Skinny Wilson asked, "Are you going to help us stupid people who can't write with the paperwork?"

"Are you wanting to get land, Skinny?"

"Yeah, Darlene is good at growing things and with that and hunting and trapping we will do well."

"I will be glad to help. It may be a good idea to pick land near each other, then you can help each other build your cabins, fight off Indians, share your cooking recipes and such."

Arco told Skinny that he had been looking at land on the river that came in from the south. They decided to ride out the next day and check it out. They took their wives with them to make sure that they liked the places they picked out. Only the trappers with wives wanted any land. Mark and Lisa Smith wanted some next to the fort. They had saved up their money and wanted to buy theirs so that they didn't have to go through the hassle connected with homesteading. Mark filled out the paperwork and bought a section thinking some day to raise cattle on it.

That same day that everyone went looking for land, Walking Buffalo talked to John about getting a ride to the Missouri River and home.

He had found an Indian saddle in the barn, John had given him a hind quarter of smoked elk to take with him and he was looking forward to leaving. Sioux country was east of the Missouri and this was Crow land and it wasn't safe for him to ride through here.

Jack Valines found land he wanted upstream from the fort, just north of Bridger Pass. It was at the edge of the forest so he wouldn't have to haul logs very far to build a cabin. It was also close enough to Blackfoot country to be safe from other tribes.

Paul Lyton decided to homestead some land just across the river to the south called the Rocky Fork. There was some forest upstream from there where he could get logs for his cabin. To homestead you had to build a cabin, plant some crops, dig a well and live there for a while. That would make it your land.

Everybody got busy. Trapping season was about to start for the year and there were four cabins to build before they all left for the winter. John said he would pay the trappers wages to help with the cabins before they left. They would need money to buy supplies for the winter anyway and if they didn't earn the money they would have to put it on their bill at the fort until spring when they brought in their furs.

After the paperwork was all done and the pieces of land were drawn on the big map the men took tools and supplies and loaded them on horses and left to start building. Arco rode the big mule that he called Samson and loaded a cross cut saw, axes and food on a pack horse and headed out. Skinny and Darlene went, too. Ella stayed at the fort with her little boy to help in the kitchen. Skinny and Darlene started building their foundation while Arco was cutting trees and dragging them in with the mule Samson to the place for Skinny's cabin. A few Crow hunters came by and watched them for a while. One of the warriors had been in the fight at the fort with the Sioux; he asked Skinny why they were building cabins on Crow land? He answered that the Crow chief said that since they had fought for the Crow against the Sioux that it was okay.

The warriors rode away. Arco asked, "Do we need to worry about this?"

"No, I think after he talks to his chief it will be alright. If not then we may have to run back to the fort. But that's the fun about living out here; there is always some excitement."

The saw millers were cutting lumber as fast as they could for floors and roofs. Two men went to the forest to cut cedar trees to make into shakes. They set up shop right outside the fort. As they made the shakes they threw them in a wagon, ready to haul to a cabin when they wanted them.

The weather turned cold by the middle of November but the cabins were all done. Skinny was a good stone mason and built each one a nice fire place. Mark was busy making furniture. A herd of Buffalo was spotted. Arco and Tom Smith and all the trappers took off for the hunt. Darlene and Dove went with Arco on the big wagon. They went to help with the skinning. Tom and Arco took rifles. They wanted to do some shooting. When they left the fort, John thought "I sure hope they don't shoot anyone."

They didn't. They actually each killed a couple of Buffalo. Some Crow hunters showed up so there were a lot of Buffalo taken that day. When they returned to the fort they put a young cow on the spits and prepared for a feast. When John saw how much meat was brought in he told Mark,

"I think we better build another smoker. If we keep getting meat like this it will start to rot before we can smoke it. And we do real well selling it from the boats; we do well on the hides too."

Mark said, "Arco said that the big team didn't like all the blood smell hauling all that meat. He said they almost ran away with the wagon; he had a lot of work handling them. Tom thought it was pretty funny. He said he had never heard a man cuss like that before."

The women had worked hard and were covered with blood and dirt when they got home. They both took baths and got all cleaned up before going to help in the kitchen. Mark had a keg of beer set up and a small keg of whiskey, too. It was fresh from the still but not bad. It would sell well at the other posts. Mr. Lyton had gone on the hunt with the rest of the men. He had never hunted before and told his wife big stories about it. He did get one Buffalo and was very excited about it. Dove had helped him skin and butcher it.

Arco and Tom loaded the smoker and got the fire going. They would have to tend the fire continually until all this meat was smoked. Tom was getting paid and knew that he would soon be rich. He would buy a better horse and exchange his trade musket for a real rifle and maybe even a set of white buckskins that fit. He was growing out of his clothes. He was almost twelve now and taller than his dad.

After dinner, John and Mark sat in the office and went over the books. John said, "Mark, you have really made this post pay. The boats are making money. I am sure the St. Louis warehouse will pay for itself eventually. I started out pretty well off but I think if all goes well and some Indian don't take my hair I will end up rich. I don't think that the fur trade will last forever and most of these little posts will close up. We will have to diversify to stay afloat."

"What do you have in mind?"

"Well, you are talking about starting a cattle ranch. I have been thinking of buying all the good farm land that the government will allow and wait for the price to go up and to sell some land and farm a lot of it."

"I can't imagine you as a farmer and it will have to wait until the Indians calm down. Of course, the Army may have that under control by the time the fur trade quits being profitable. People will still want to travel on the boats and ship produce and equipment so they will continue to do well. Do you plan to stay around here after you're rich?"

"Yes, I thought about going back to Boston but I would miss the west and you and Lisa and the kids."

Arco hooked up Samson to the light wagon and loaded up the furniture that Mark made for them. He then helped Ella and little John up to the wagon seat and drove out to the new cabin. Ella helped him move all the furniture into the house and made lunch. While they ate she looked at Arco and said, "Do you remember the day John bought us and I prayed and thanked God for nice white people? You weren't sure I was right. What do you think now?"

"You were right. John and Margaret and Mark and Lisa have been real good to us. I thanks God for them every day." After lunch they went back to the fort. Arco had to haul and split wood for the smoker and take his shift at keeping the fire going. He was thinking about building a barn and corrals. Skinny said he had a good plan and they could work together. Darlene stayed at the fort to have her baby. It was a girl; they named her Karen.

The Frog was loaded with fur packs and smoked meat to sell down river. Walking Buffalo went aboard with two horses, John gave him another for a pack horse. And the boat sailed.

Jack Valines and Dove went to visit Lame Wolf and her mom to show off their new baby and to invite them to come see their new house.

Margaret went into labor and John did his pacing up and down in his office. He missed dinner and kept up the pacing half the night until Dove came in the room, "You have another son. Your wife is fine. Everybody is sleeping so go sleep in the bunk house. We are still cleaning up at your house. She said his name is Wayne."

Lisa could not let Dove and Margaret get ahead of her so she also went into labor. She had another girl they named Sue. Mark came in and said, "A lot of material had come in on the Frog and the women are all busy making baby clothes.

We won't make any money on that cloth. They are just helping themselves and not offering to pay a penny."

John laughed. "Did you ask any of them to pay?"

"I asked my wife. She said if I have to pay you won't get any pie or cookies or cake until spring. I backed down fast."

"I don't think I'll mention it to any of them. We had better get some firewood; winter is on the way. By the way, I ordered some steel from England to be brought to St. Louis in the spring. Mr. Lyons will be able to make axes and knives to sell the Indians and trappers. We will sell it to him at just a small percent above our cost so that he can make a good profit. Did you charge anything for the furniture you made for the cabins? The lumber is free but we should get something for your labor."

"I pay those guys to cut the lumber. Beside, you get twenty five percent of everything."

"I put it on their bills. By the way who is paying their bills?"

"I keep track of the time they work for us. So I guess I am taking care of their bills. I will get the book and we can settle up."

Mark said, "Arco and Tom are real busy at the smoker and running the still. It's hard to get the little Frenchman to do much other than drink. I think you should put him to cutting firewood. At least he could drive the team to drag in logs. I don't know if I would trust him with an ax. I am going to put my second son, Bill, to helping Tom and Arco keep the fires going. He needs something to keep him busy and out of trouble. Put him in your book; it's time he did some work."

CHAPTER EIGHTEEN
THE SECOND WINTER

By Thanksgiving the firewood was all in and stacked by the cabins. Arco and Tom and Bill went hunting, Bill for the first time. They found a trail through the woods west of Arco's cabin that showed the tracks of deer and elk; they set up a blind and waited. Bill shot a doe and Arco helped him carry it to his cabin and showed him how to dress it. Tom got a young bull elk, drug it behind his horse to the cabin where they skinned and cut it up to haul back to the fort and get it in the smoker along with Bill's doe. All the buffalo from the big hunt was smoked and put in the storage buildings.

With all the supplies in the store room and the smoked meat in storage they were ready for winter. The women had plenty of cloth to keep them busy sewing for the winter so everybody was happy.

Mark put Bill to work in the store, stocking shelves and learning the books. He was better than Tom at the books. Tom was busy at the still and trappers were still bringing in meat to be smoked so he was working at the smoker too. Mark was making baby furniture in his spare time. Arco and Laville were sawing lumber and fire wood so everyone was busy and getting ready for Christmas. John and Mark were making little wooden toys for the kids. John was good at carving dolls and kitchen things and Mark believed that it would sell in the store. The Indians liked that stuff for their kids too.

Margaret came to John's office one day just to visit. She brought the boys; she wanted to talk. He asked, "How are things with the women?"

"We are all doing well, but we need a break. How about you calling a holiday? Send some one out to get a couple of turkeys and maybe some ducks."

"That just makes more work for you, getting everything ready for a feast."

"That's true, but it's a break from the regular routine." The baby started fussing a little and she unbuttoned her dress to nurse him. John was a little shocked that she would do it right there in his office, but she acted like it was no big thing. She didn't even cover up with his blanket so he was looking at her other breast while she kept talking about the dinner. He didn't complain about the view but it was hard to concentrate on what she was saying. When she had told him all her plans and what she wanted him to do, she left. He realized that he was thinking more about her breasts than about what she had said. He put it out of his mind and went back to work on his books.

Some Crows came to trade and one of them asked Mark about the cabins that went up on their land. They wanted to know who gave permission to build there. John decided to go visit the Crow chief and make sure that all was well. If they got mad about cabins they would all be in trouble.

John could do sign language as well as anyone but he took a trapper who spoke the language to interpret for him. The main Crow village was only a day's ride from them so they left before daylight so that they could be there before dark. About noon they ran into some hunters on the way home and rode along with them into the village. They went to the teepee of one of the hunters to wait to be presented to the Chief.

It had to be done just so or one would be in trouble. They had to do a big feast and a council fire. It took about an hour. The hunter got word that all was ready and led them to the council fire. John had brought tobacco and gun powder for gifts for the Chief. They were seated and introduced to Chief Tall Elk and gave him the gifts.

Tall Elk thanked him for the gifts and asked how the new fort was doing. John replied, "We are doing well. We just got a boat load of new things to sell. You should come see." Tall Elk just grunted then made a long speech about the time some Crow families had fought with this hairy face against the Sioux and how the Sioux had lost fifty warriors and the Crow had only lost one. He went on about the bravery of the Crow and what great fighters they were and how they had saved the fort from the Sioux. The trapper who spoke Crow was Flanagan. He translated Tall Elk's talk and John had to try hard not to smile at Tall Elk's tall tale. After they ate some buffalo stew John got a chance to talk to the chief about building cabins on Crow land. Tall Elk knew about the cabins. He instructed John to ask first from now on. He said that he couldn't stop the Sioux or the Blackfoot from burning down the cabins. He couldn't protect them. John told him to come by the fort and he would give him a new knife that the blacksmith had made. He could pick out one that he liked. They talked about going hunting together and when the counsel broke up they went to bed in an empty teepee. At first light they left for home.

Everyone who could went out and cut hay for the winter; they used both wagons to haul it to the barn. Old Coonskin said it was going to start snowing heavy and they needed a lot of hay to last the winter. Even John and Mark went out and helped while Bill watched the store. It wasn't long after the last load of hay was in that it started to snow. It didn't look like it would quit until spring. When Christmas got there John and Mark had finished plenty of toys for the little children. The older boys got new guns. Tom asked John, "Can you scare up an Indian attack so we can use our new rifles?"

"No the Indians are too busy having Christmas dinner to come fight."

The women made a lot of clothes for presents for everyone. Mark complained that they didn't pay for the cloth. John asked, "Did you ask Lisa to pay for what she took?"

"No. I like to eat and don't want to sleep in the bunkhouse."

John laughed. "I didn't ask my wife either."

Christmas day came right on schedule; it was still snowing. He asked the boys to shovel walks between the buildings first thing in the morning so people could go back and forth with ease.

All of the presents were under the big tree in the mess hall. So it was agreed that everyone would come open presents after breakfast. There was no wrapping paper back then so most of the gifts were just put under the tree during the night with a little tag saying who it was for. Some were wrapped in cloth. The children made sure everybody was up early. Breakfast was served in the dining hall, the same hall where all those presents were so the kids of all ages were excited to get to them. There was something there for everyone, even the old drunk Deville got a new shirt with a note that said it was from Santa.

Jack and Dove and the boys came down the river in a canoe the day before Christmas. Skinny and Darlene with Karen had ridden in the day before. Margaret told everyone that Jack would pass out the gifts so there wasn't a scramble at the tree. When all the presents were handed out Margaret told all the kids that she would write to Santa thanking him for all the great things that he had sent. The women went to start cooking the Christmas dinner and baking cookies and pies. The men sat around the table drinking coffee and telling lies and watching the kids play.

The quiet of Christmas day was shattered when a shot was fired from the walls by a sentry. The men all grabbed their weapons and ran out and climbed the catwalks. The sentry said about twenty Sioux had crossed the river to the south and were coming to visit and he didn't know if they were hostile or not. John looked through his telescope. "They are not wearing war paint but they are not packing fur packs on pack horses either. That looks like Walking Buffalo leading them. Maybe it is peaceful." When Walking Buffalo rode up to within yelling distance, Leville, who spoke Sioux, called to him, "Walking Buffalo, did you come to trade or fight?"

"We came to smoke a pipe with John and to trade."

"What do you have to trade?"

"Some Crow squaws we caught."

"Are they alive and in good shape or half dead?"

"They are in good shape."

Where are they? We don't see them?" Walking Buffalo turned and spoke to a man beside him. The man rode back to the river and yelled and three warriors rode to the river and crossed. Each one had a squaw riding with them. John asked Leville, "What do they want for them?"

Walking Buffalo said, "Me know that you have a lot of smoked buffalo. Give us one quarter for each squaw. We need meat." John signed to him to bring the squaws around to the gate and wait. He would bring out the meat. He told Arco to get two of the worst looking ponies, load two quarters on each and come stand by while he took them out to Walking Buffalo. The men went to the catwalk above the gate to watch as Arco opened the gate and John led the two ponies out and the squaws back in.

Darlene spoke Crow and came to the gate to get the squaws and take them to the dining hall to get warmed and fed. Everyone around wanted to know what happened and how they were captured. They said they were in the woods getting firewood when the Sioux snuck up on them and grabbed them. The Sioux had come to steal horses but the herd was too well guarded to suit them. The women believed their people would be coming after them. It would not be hard to follow the tracks in the snow.

Darlene asked, "Shall we wait for them to come get you or take you back right away?"

"It would look better if you took us back. It would not look like you were planning to keep us that way or that you were going to sell us in your store." Mark had built a sled for hauling firewood so Skinny Wilson hooked Samson to it and piled some hay in it. They took off first thing in the morning with the three squaws wrapped in new blankets that Mark gave them. They met the Crow warriors about half way. The Crow just turned and followed the sled to their village. The squaws told the warriors what had happened so they let Arco turn around and head back. It would take him half the night but he was glad to go. There were a lot of Indians in that village and it made him nervous. If Samson knew that Indians like to eat mule meat he would have run all the way back. It all made for an exciting Christmas.

A week later Tall Elk with a few other Crow came to trade. One of the Christmas squaws was with them. She was his younger sister. John showed him the knives that Lyton made there at the fort. John told him to pick one to keep as a gift for letting them build on Crow land. Tall Elk thanked him for sending his sister and the other girls back. The Crow spent the night and left early. John watched from the wall as they rode off. When they crossed the river to the south he saw a group of about twenty warriors waiting for them.

John went to the store to tell Mark. They were both worried about Tall Elk getting home safely. There might still be some Sioux hanging around.

A group of trappers came in to trade their first bundles of winter fur for supplies. Mark told them that the fort was having a big New Year's Eve party that they were welcome to attend. There would be a lot to eat and plenty to drink and music and dancing. They just had to make sure that they didn't get rough with the girls. Coonskin was there; "Don't worry. I'll make sure they are good boys and that they mind their manners."

Coonskin and Deville started a fire in the barbeque pit and put half an elk on to cook. There were two turkeys and some fish from the river and don't forget the pies and cakes and cookies. There was a barrel of beer and one of hard cider and a keg of whiskey seasoned in the barrel for two weeks.

By the time the food was ready all the men had whetted their appetites and were feeling mellow. The music started right after dinner. Coonskin asked Margaret to dance and that started the dancing. Everybody danced with their wives and the trappers danced with each other. At midnight everybody yelled Happy New Year and John had one of the swivel guns fired. A lot of guns were popping. By three in the morning only the sentries on the walls were still awake.

It was January first of the second year at Fort Brixton and all seemed well. Mark and John were in the office working on the books when Mark said, "We need to rework the book of our cost per item because it's costing less shipping direct to St. Louis. What do you think?"

"I think we should wait to see how much less before we change anything. We have enough work to do keeping up with the books for three stores, two steamboats and wages for all the people working for us. And for how much you ding me for all the stuff my wife steals from you. I guess it's not stealing if I pay the bill."

That's a big if. Do you do the books for the Boston store?"

"No, Mr. Park does them but he sends me copies. I have to go over them and enter the bottom line into the Company books. I need help."

"Maybe you could get Mrs. Lyton to help you. She is the only woman without babies to care for or maybe she could watch your kids and Margaret could do it.

"That's a good idea. I'll talk to them and see if we can work something out."

John met with the two women. Mrs. Lyton declined, "I wouldn't be any good with your books but I would be happy to watch your boys so that Margaret can work with you."

"Thank you, Mrs. Lyton, I need some help although it worries me a little for Margaret to know how much money we have. She will want to spend a lot more."

It took two weeks for Margaret to learn the books for the fort. She had very little schooling.

She was good with numbers but her spelling was very bad. She could read but not well and John's writing was sometimes hard for her to decipher. The book showing all the products that they sold and the cost for each item took a long time for her to get. At home one night she said, "Thank you for being patient with me. You are so good at this stuff that you probably think I'm an idiot. You should have married someone better educated than me."

"I married you for your beauty and because I fell in love with you. And you are learning very fast and will be a big help. It is also nice to have a pretty woman to look at every day while I work."

Coonskin and the group he trapped with came in with fur packs to trade for supplies. He stopped by the office and when he saw Margaret he remarked, "Well, it is about time you hired some good looking help around here."

"Thank you, Coonskin. You were in not long ago; did you run out of whiskey already?"

"No, I ran out of coffee. I didn't get enough last time. I also just wanted to see your pretty face again. It gives me hope that if I save my money that someday I will be able to go down the river and find me a pretty woman like you." John entered the conversation, "As ugly as you are you will have to save a lot more than you make trapping fur."

"Maybe I will just shoot you and steal Margaret." They were all smiling by then.

A group of Black Foot from Lame Wolf's village rode to the other side of the river; they walked across on the ice carrying their fur packs to trade for tobacco and gun powder and lead. Old Lame Wolf told them not to buy whiskey. Mark ask them why they didn't ride across the river.

They said they tried that once and lost a horse. The sharp hooves broke the ice and in it went.

As soon as the Black Foots left a large group of Crow showed up. They had been waiting across the river to the south until the others were gone. They had some women with them and wanted to trade for some sugar and salt and tobacco. The squaws wanted some beads and some mirrors. The men also bought some whiskey. All the trading was peaceful.

When the end of January arrived the trappers and groups of Indians started coming in to trade. The warehouse was filling up with fur packs and Arco said that they were running out of whiskey bottles. He told Mark to ask the trappers to bring back their empties to refill. Mr. Lyton was busy shoeing horses and making knives and axes. Mark told him that he needed to eat more because the fort owed him more than he owed them.

Some free trappers came in and told Mark that the Indians had made it hot for them and they hadn't been able to hunt and they were hungry. They traded for two smoked buffalo quarters, some dried vegetables and other food. They had spent the winter in the Bitter Root Mountains where the trapping was good but they had been dodging Shoshones all winter as they were not friendly. They had lost one man and had two more wounded.

Margaret told John that she and Ella and Dove were all pregnant again. He responded, "I think we had better either build a bigger fort or pass a law against you girls getting yourselves that way."

"I've said it before and I'll say it again: you guys should learn the facts of life."

The river didn't break up until the middle of April. The Shannon showed up a week later loaded to the rafters with supplies. And some bad news. Mr. George Grey had come down with a fever and they needed help. Mrs. Grey couldn't handle it all. She had help in the warehouse and used Mr. Jorgenson in the store when she needed him but she couldn't do the books too. John and Margaret, Lisa and Mark and Captain Small met in the salon on the boat. The Captain said, "The store is doing real well. Your prices are reasonable and your merchandise is good. But they haven't been able to find good help for the store. It seems like anybody who is out of work can't read and write. I think one of you should go down there and help out until you can maybe get someone from back east or maybe New Orleans."

Margaret said, "John is the only one who knows how to do all the books. But if he goes it might take a while so the boys and I would like to go too." Mark said, "My wife and I would like to go too but we all know we can't all go and Rendezvous is not far off. Someone needs to go to that. We can't send one of the trappers; they can't read and write. They would probably get drunk and give away all the merchandise." They laughed but it was kind of strained. John thought for a moment, "Maybe we should sell out and all go. I have had offers. It's a good profitable business."

Mark said, "I would like to buy it but I don't have a lot of money. Maybe we could work out some time payments or something. I know that you have put in a lot of money making it pay and I could not begin to pay that much for it. The biggest thing would be that we would miss you a lot if you left. We have been through a lot since we met."

The Captain told them to cut it out. "You are going to make me cry. If you do this, are you going to sell the boats too?"

"Why, are you getting tired of running the river and want to quit on me? To answer your question: no. We need the boats. The fort would be cut off here without supplies. Well, I will have to think about it and talk it over with Margaret. The decision has to be made quickly so Margaret and I will go talk about it now. We will let you know."

When they got home John asked her, "Well, what do you think?"

"I would like to move away from the wilderness. I would like to spend some of your money and not worry about Indian attacks and being scalped. I would like to live where the boys can go to a good school. I would like to have our next baby in a hospital and not on a table in the mess hall. Those things are on the plus side. The other side is I will miss everybody here and will cry a lot when we leave here. I will even miss the loud cussing of the trappers. I won't miss the smell of the place and the Indians. Does that answer your question?"

John and Mark worked out a payment plan. John made it easy for him. They had a huge going away party. John and Margaret both made nice speeches about how much they were going to miss everyone and they all shed a few tears and all the men had too much to drink. Even John got a little tipsy and kissed Lisa and Dove and Ella. Arco asked if he and Ella were going with them. John said, "You are not slaves anymore and you own land and both have jobs here. You are safe from slave catchers here. Don't you like it here?"

"Yes sir, but I sometimes forgets that I'm not a slave anymore. Thank you for all you have done for us. We will always pray for you, sir."

"And we will pray for you too, Arco. I want to wish you a lot of luck too."

Once the Shannon was loaded with fur packs and hides and smoked meat to sell down river, John and Margaret and the boys said their goodbyes and went aboard. They left most of their things behind, thinking they would buy new clothes and things in St. Louis. John took his horse and money and gun but not much else. They stopped at all the posts on the way down river to pick up passengers and freight but they made good time.

They met the Frog on the way and stopped for the night to go over the books with Ned Jones. He said that another ship from England had come in since the Shannon had sailed so he had a full load of supplies for Fort Brixton. John told him that Mark had bought it from him so he would have to sell the load to him. They went over the lists and John told him how much he should get for it. The Captain warned that this was going to make more work for him and he had enough to do already.

"I will give you a raise and I think you two Captains should hire a clerk to ride with you to do the paperwork."

When they reached St. Louis, John asked the teamster Stacy Cunningham to drive Margaret around looking at houses for sale while he went to work. Mr. Grey was getting better but still not able to work. Mr. Cunningham's wife was working as a clerk in the store now; with John there things went well. Margaret found a house to rent and had Stacy drive her around buying furniture, at least enough so they could stay there when the boat sailed back up the river.

The ship from England was still loading fur and hides so the Shannon tied up beside her and unloaded direct into her. Some of the supplies from England were loaded directly into the

Shannon to take up river. John had Captain Small give them some smoked buffalo to eat on the way home.

This is getting to the end of the story. John bought a small farm a few miles up river from St. Louis with a small cabin on it. He ended up renting the cabin out to a sharecropper and having a house built on the bluff overlooking the Mississippi. He bought Margaret a closed one horse carriage to go shopping in and rode his horse to the warehouse every day. They went to the little Baptist church every Sunday and became great friends with Rev. Johnson and his family. Mark and Lisa and Fort Brixton did well and they all lived happily ever after.

THE END

www.ingramcontent.com/pod-product-compliance
Lightning Source LLC
Chambersburg PA
CBHW072150070526
44585CB00015B/1071